Midnight Writings
By The Ole Bishop

Bobby Johnson

All Scripture passages are taken from the
King James Version of the Holy Bible.

ISBN: 9798394351525

Dedication

I dedicate this book to the following:

My Parents
Simon B. and Lillie Mae Johnson

And

Phyllis' Parents
Charles and Irene Menke

Acknowledgments

My Appreciation is expressed to the following
for their participation in the creation of this book:

My Wife, Phyllis

My Daughter, Charlene Hardin

Gerald Funderburk

Tommy Harvey

Patsy Padgett - For her many hours of labor
to bring this book to completion

Table of Contents

Dedication

Acknowledgments

Meditations

Sermon Thoughts

Funeral Sermons

Excerpts from Funeral Sermons

Special Features

Closing – By the Ole Bishop | 185

Foreword

Midnight Writings By The Ole Bishop was written mostly around midnight. Phyllis, my wife, and I usually watch a movie each night and retire to the bedroom rather late.

After sixty-five years of full-time ministry, I feel that I have some information to share. Although I attended three colleges, earning a Bachelor of Arts Degree from Coker College in 1969 and making an 'A' on my State Teacher's Exam, preparation was more in the teaching field than in ministry.

In my first book, *"Taking a Chance With God,"* I wrote, "I attended Clemson University one day and made an 'A' – that was on the State Teacher's Exam.

Many of you have read my first book. I feel that my ministry was begun and has continued in the same manner of *"Taking A Chance With God."* I am an Ordained Bishop in the Church of God. I have adhered faithfully to the teachings and doctrines of the church. I have supported the church financially beyond measure, but I have not been restricted by my denomination. No minister should be restricted by a denomination.

The theme for our 2023 Annual Convention is "Dare to Dream." I have *'dared to dream.'* I have followed my dreams. I have not been afraid or intimidated to follow them. They have been fulfilled. I encourage you to get my book, *"Taking A Chance With God."* As the prophets of yesteryear and the apostles of yesterday, I feel that I have followed the Lord in my ministry and now in my writings.

I hope and pray that you will be blessed by my sermons, my helps, and the inspired features in this book. Surely there is a needed sermon, a helpful thought, or an inspired feature in this book for you.

There have been times during these writings that my heart has pounded in my chest; that my tears have filled my eyes; and, that my spirit has been stirred. Now, I encourage you to read this book – to *Dare to Dream* – to follow your dream, and, to write your own book.

Well, it is around midnight, May 7, 2023, and Phyllis thinks it is time to retire for the night. So, the Ole Bishop will say, "Good Night, Good Night."

Part I

Some Favorite Messages

Chapter 1

What A Scene!

What a scene - when that host of beautiful angels flew around Bethlehem and announced to the humble shepherds that the Christ of Glory had been born. Luke 2:11 *"For unto you is born this day in the city of David, a Saviour, which is Christ the Lord."*

What a scene! It was when John the Baptist stood on the banks of the Jordan River with his black mane hanging down on his shoulders, dressed in camel skin and a leather girdle about his waist, eating honey and grasshoppers, and shouting with a loud voice, *"Repent! Repent!"* Matthew 3:1-2. The merchants in Jerusalem closed their stores, the doctors ceased their practice, the attorneys left their offices, the carpenters laid down their tools, the mechanics laid aside their wrenches, the farmers stopped their plowing, the housewives left their kitchens, and all the country turned out and headed to the banks of the Jordan to hear a strange man, dressed in a strange outfit, preaching a strange message – *"Repent! Repent!"* Matthew 3:1-6.

What a scene! It was according to John, Chapter 9, when Jesus saw a man blind from birth. My, my, my, what a scene as He approached the blind man. He spat on the ground, made clay of the spittle, and anointed the eyes of the blind man with the clay. Then said unto him, *"Go, wash in the pool of Siloam."* Can you imagine what the disciples and by-standers were saying? Verse 7 - He went his way, he washed, and he came seeing! Oh! Oh! Oh! Have you heard the story of the blind man? What a scene!!!

What a scene! As recorded in Mark, Chapter 2, as Christ ministered in a Capernaum house. It was <u>noised</u> that He was in the house. <u>Many</u> were gathered together. The words were spoken, "No room for anyone else – even as about the door." <u>Look at it!</u> Four men carrying a sick sinner on a bed. No room to enter – what a jam!

Verse 4 - *"And when they could not come nigh unto him for the press, they uncovered the roof where he was: and when they had broken it up, they let down the bed wherein the sick of the palsy lay."* <u>Get Ready!</u> There is a way to Jesus – He Is The Way!

Verse 5 – *"When Jesus saw their faith, he said unto the sick of the palsy, Son, thy sins be forgiven thee."* Then Jesus was questioned and criticized. After which He said unto the man, *"Arise!"* Glory! <u>Arise</u> (somebody needs to arise). *"Take up your bed and walk."* Somebody needs to walk! Do you want a miracle? <u>Then Arise – Now Walk.</u>

Verse 12 – *"And immediately he arose, took up the bed."* He walked! <u>What A Scene!</u>

What a scene! When the Lord Jesus Christ was nailed to the cross and it was suspended between earth and heaven as the sun withdrew its light, as the veil of the Temple was rent from the top to the bottom, as the earth quaked and screams filled the air and dead saints walked about.

Glory! Glory! Glory! What a Scene!

What a scene when that same Jesus arose from the dead, came forth out of the tomb, rattling the keys of death and hell, saying, *"I am He that liveth and was dead. Now I am alive and I have the keys."* What a scene! <u>He Is Alive!</u>

His Resurrection is the greatest proof of the Gospel.

His Resurrection is the greatest evidence of Christianity.

His Resurrection is the greatest exhibition of God's Power.

His Resurrection is the greatest reality of Faith.

His Resurrection is the greatest assurance of His Second Coming.

His Resurrection is the greatest confirmation of our Hope.

Titus 2:11 – *"For the grace of God that bringeth salvation hath appeared to all men."* Does anyone feel like shouting???

What a scene! It was when He took the disciples out to Bethany, lifted up His hands, and blessed them – telling them <u>where</u> to go and <u>what</u> to do, then making His glorious ascension to Heaven.

Listen! No mortal tongue has been able to explain such a scene. No artist has been able to paint the scene. No eyes have been able to fully behold the scene. No mind of man has been able to grasp the scene.

What a scene as we turn to Acts 2:2-4 when the Holy Ghost came down on the Day of Pentecost. The disciples and others, in obedience to Jesus, went to the Upper Room (a designated room in Jerusalem) and waited for the fulfillment of the <u>Promise.</u>

"And suddenly there came a sound from heaven as of a rushing mighty wind, and it filled all the house where they were sitting. 3 And there appeared unto them cloven tongues like as of fire, and it sat upon each of them. 4 And they were all filled with the Holy Ghost, and began to speak with other tongues, as the Spirit gave them utterance."

What a Scene!

Now, let us go to 1 Thessalonians 4:16-18, *"For the Lord himself shall descend from heaven with a shout, with the voice of the archangel, and with the trump of God: and the dead in Christ shall rise first: 17 Then we which are alive and remain shall be caught up together with them in the clouds, to meet the Lord in the air: and so shall we ever be with the Lord. 18 Wherefore comfort one another with these words."*

Oh! What a Scene! When the blest who sleep in Jesus at His bidding shall arise, from the silence of the grave and from the sea, when from every climate and nation He shall call His people home, what a gathering of the ransomed that will be. Graves all bursting – Saints all shouting!

- That shout will break the silence of the ages.
- The sound of the trumpet – 1 Corinthians 15:52 *"In a moment, in the twinkling of an eye, at the last trump: for the trumpet shall sound, and the dead shall be raised incorruptible, and we shall be changed."* Hear the Apostle Paul again, *"Behold, I shew you a mystery; We shall not all sleep, but we shall all be changed."* 1 Corinthians 15:51.
- Oh Joy! Oh Delight! Should we go without dying.
- No sickness, no sadness, no dread and no crying.
- Caught up through the clouds to meet the Lord in Heavenly Glory when Jesus receives His own.

To be with Him Forever!
So, comfort one another with this scene . . .
What a Scene!
What A Day that Will Be!!!

Chapter 2

I Don't Want to Get Adjusted

There is an ole song that is recorded in the Church Hymnal, "I Don't Want to Get Adjusted."

I don't want to get adjusted to this world, to this world.

I've got a home that's so much better.

I'm gonna go there sooner or later,

And I don't want to get adjusted to this world.

When I consider the present-day crisis, the song rings out, "I don't want to get adjusted to this world."

When I consider the devastation, the desolation, and the despair of today, the song rings out, "I don't want to get adjusted to this world."

When I consider the corruption in our political system, "I don't want to get adjusted to this world."

When I consider the conflicts among countries, "I don't want to get adjusted to this world."

When I turn to the Weather Channel and see the destruction made by tornadoes, hurricanes, earthquakes, and floods, the song comes to my mind, "I don't want to get adjusted to this world."

When I think about the ravaging results of sin and sinning, the ole song rings out, "I don't want to get adjusted to this world."

When I hear about the affliction and diseases that are affecting so many of us, the ole song rings out, "I don't want to get adjusted to this world."

When I read 1 John 2:15-17, *"Love not the world, neither the things that are in the world. If any man love the world, the love of the Father is not in him. 16 For all that is in the world, the lust of the flesh, and the lust of the eyes, and the pride of life, is not of the Father, but is of the world. 17 And the world passeth away, and the lust thereof: but he that doeth the will of God abideth for ever."* - I am ready to sing, "I don't want to get adjusted to this world."

When I read Psalms 39:4-6, *"LORD, make me to know mine end, and the measure of my days, what it is; that I may know how frail I am. 5 Behold, thou hast made my days as an handbreadth; and mine age is as nothing before thee: verily every man at his best state is altogether vanity. Selah. 6 Surely every man walketh in a vain shew: surely they are disquieted in vain: he heapeth up riches, and knoweth not who shall gather them,"* I am reminded of: the Frailty of Life, the Vanity of Life, the Brevity of Life, and the Uncertainty of Life; and, I am ready to burst forth, "I don't want to get adjusted to this world!!!"

The song rings out when I read in the Book of Revelation . . .

- Chapter 6:12-14: The opening of the sixth seal, the great earthquake, sun as black as sackcloth, the moon as blood, stars falling, islands moving out of their place;

- Chapter 8: Voices, thunderings, flashes of lightning, an earthquake, hail, and fire mingled with blood, trees burnt, and all green grass burnt;
- Chapter 9: Men seeking death and not able to find it, and, the sting of scorpions.

It is no wonder that Paul wrote in Colossians 3:1-4, "*If ye then be risen with Christ, <u>seek those things which are above</u>, where Christ sitteth on the right hand of God. ² <u>Set your affection on things above, not on things on the earth</u>. ³ For ye are dead, and your life is hid with Christ in God. ⁴ When Christ, who is our life, shall appear, then shall ye also appear with him in glory.*"

Listen! Everything around us proclaims the transitory nature of things below! As believers in the Lord Jesus Christ, we should set our affections on things above.

- o This world is not suited for our residence.
- o It is not the place of our eternal destination.
- o It is not the scene of our eternal repose.

Let me say . . .
Thank God for Life. . .
The Blessings of Life. . .
The Privileges of Life. . .
The Opportunities of Life. . .
Even, the Challenges of Life!

Unfortunately, too many of us prefer the present to the future. Too many of us are absorbed too much in the fleeting scenes of this life. Too many of us are living and acting as if this world, this earth, is our highest and final destination. May we not belittle what the Lord has made for us, what He has provided, what He has given us. . . to enable us to make our journey through this life.

Hear Psalm 33:15 *". . . the earth is full of the goodness of the LORD."*

Hear Psalm 115:16 *"The heaven, even the heavens, are the LORD'S: but the earth hath he given to the children of men."*

Hear Genesis 1:1 *"In the beginning God created the heaven and the earth."* Vs.3-4 *"And God said, Let there be light: and there was light. And God saw the light, that it was good."*

After each phase of God's creation, the Bible said, "And God saw that it was good." The summary is found in Genesis 1:31, *"And God saw every thing that he had made, and, behold, it was very good."*

Oh! But sin entered!!! Satan raised up his head! Man fell! Sin worked its ravaging ways!!! The whole world was affected by his destructive power causing: Devastation – Desolation – Destruction. Sorrow, Heartache, Pain, and Death seem to be the order of each day.

However, <u>there **is** a song</u> for believers -

"This world is not my home. I'm only passing by.
My treasures and my hope are all up in the sky."

Glory!!!

Our eternal hope is above –
There is the abode of peace and purity
Suffering and sorrow cannot enter

Temptation has no power, No sad goodbyes
It will be <u>Wonderful There</u>!

Let me tell you again - The things down here cannot satisfy the soul, they are unsuited to it, they are beneath it. This world is not suited to your disposition – not suited – not suited – not suited! It cannot answer your expectations. It cannot fulfill your hopes.

Our possession is on the other side of Jordan. Heaven. Happy Home Above. Heaven - where there is peace and love. What a Place!

God:

- o Who is a Lover of beauty, painted the butterfly's wing
- o Put the red on the Robin's Breast
- o Threw the Drapery of a thousand colors around the evening Sun
- o Gave the Rose its blushing charm
- o Touched the Lily with its dreamy white, and
- o Placed the Rainbow with its elegance in the sky.

But He, the Lord God, spared nothing in majesty composition when He created Heaven the Home of the Redeemed. Are you redeemed?

I have a home prepared where the saints abide! Just over in the Glory Land Way!!!

Chapter 3

Holding Fast the Profession of Our Faith

Hebrews 10:23 *"Let us hold fast the profession of our faith without wavering; (for he is faithful that promised)."*

There are so many faithful people in my life and ministry that I cannot write about all of them individually, but tonight my mind is absolutely flooded with them. Therefore, I am writing this message right now as I think about them on this cold December night, December 13, 2023.

The profession of a person's faith is a Christian profession and experience. Paul writes, *"Hold fast."* Why, Paul, have you made such an admonition? The answer to Paul's question is answered in the first chapter of Peter's Epistle and the first chapter of James' Epistle. Both writers inform us that our faith (our profession and our experience) will be tried.

A Christian's faith can be tried by this world system which includes temptations, tribulations, and unrighteousness. A Christian's faith can be tried by family, companions, children, sickness, afflictions, and death. A Christian's faith can be tried even by the church, its affairs, and its operation.

Timothy, in his writings, speaks often about the trying of man's faith. Here are some of them:
- 1 Timothy 4:1 *"Now the Spirit speaketh expressly, that in the latter times some shall*

depart from the faith, *giving heed to seducing spirits, and doctrines of devils."*
- o 1 Timothy 5:8 *"But if any provide not for his own, and specially for those of his own house, he hath denied the faith, and is worse than an infidel."*
- o 2 Timothy 2:18 *"Who concerning the truth have erred, saying that the resurrection is past already; and overthrow the faith of some."*

I thank God for the many, many believers on my mind tonight who did not depart from the faith, who did not deny the faith, who did not detour from the faith, but instead, kept the faith and could testify before leaving this old world:

2 Timothy 4:6-7 *"For I am now ready to be offered, and the time of my departure is at hand. ⁷ I have fought a good fight, I have finished my course, I have kept the faith."*

As recorded in Acts 14:22, *"they continued in the faith."*
As recorded in 1 Timothy, *"they fought the good right of faith."*
As recorded in Jude 3, *"they contended for the faith."*

Glory! They had "decision of character," a complete surrender to the Lord: no half-heartedness and no lukewarmness.

They had "constancy of spirit." Their heart was fixed; their mind was established; their soul stayed on the Lord.

They had "perseverance in practice." They walked in love; they prayed in the spirit; they abounded in good works.

As I sit at my desk tonight trying to finish this message before Midnight, there are so many of these wonderful believers on my mind: such as the Emanuels, at my first church, the Latta Church of God; Sister Minnie Lane and her prayer group at the Mullins Church of God; the Hunts at New Ellenton; Eunice Clardy at Liberty; Bennie Parker at Florence; and Dorothy Howard and others who prayed at the Greer Church of God.

Then, my mind became absolutely flooded with the many early members who took a chance with the new church and were faithful unto death. Many of their children and grands are still faithful to Praise Cathedral, too many to list.

In closing, consider Hebrews 12:1-2:

"Wherefore seeing we also are compassed about with so great a cloud of witnesses, let us lay aside every weight, and the sin which doth so easily beset us, and let us run with patience the race that is set before us,

2 Looking unto Jesus the author and finisher of our faith; who for the joy that was set before him endured the cross, despising the shame, and is set down at the right hand of the throne of God."

Chapter 4

When God Became Man

Hebrews 2:14-16 *"Forasmuch then as the children are partakers of flesh and blood, he also himself likewise took part of the same; that through death he might destroy him that had the power of death, that is, the devil;*

15 And deliver them who through fear of death were all their lifetime subject to bondage. 16 For verily he took not on him the nature of angels; but he took on him the seed of Abraham."

One of the most glorious happenings of all time is:
- when God became a man;
- when God formed Himself into a man;
- when God put on our humanity;
- when God took upon Himself our nature;
- when God became tabernacled in the flesh;
- oh yes, when a body was prepared for Him;
- oh yes, when He became the Son of Man;
- and yes, when He became our Brother.

By the assumption of our nature, He became our Brother. Our Brother on whom devolved the right to redeem back His enslaved kinsmen, who were lost and undone.

Psalm 142:4 *"I looked on my right hand, and beheld, but there was no man that would know me: refuge failed me; no man cared for my soul."*

That has to be one of the saddest thoughts that a person can have – no man knows me, that is, no man acknowledges me, no man recognizes me, no man cares for me, no man to help me!

Revelation 5:1-4 *"And I saw in the right hand of him that sat on the throne a book written within and on the backside, sealed with seven seals.*

² And I saw a strong angel proclaiming with a loud voice, Who is worthy to open the book, and to loose the seals thereof?

³ And no man in heaven, nor in earth, neither under the earth, was able to open the book, neither to look thereon.

⁴ And I wept much, because no man was found worthy to open and to read the book, neither to look thereon."

No man was worthy. No man was able. May I impress upon you the utter inadequacy of human means to heal and to deliver sin sick man. If earthly power had been sufficient, God could have raised up a great hero for the weak. God could have given wisdom, as to Solomon. God could have given meekness and endurance, as to Moses. God could have given courage, as to Joshua and David. God could have given physical strength, as to Samson.

But all would have been mere feebleness in regard to a work so stupendous as man's redemption, as to man's deliverance, as to man's healing.

In all the millions of humanity, there has been no one to interpose, no one to redeem, no advocate to heal, and no one to deliver, except Jesus Christ, our Lord.

Every man born, except the Lord Jesus Christ, has been involved in the same common condemnation and misery. He was without sin. He knew no sin. There was no other. No other! This is brought out in Isaiah, Chapter 59, as Israel's iniquities are listed. After this, the writer points out in Verse 16 that he saw no man to help and wondered that there was no intercessor.

But God, in His mercy and love, remembered man who was in moral darkness, who was helpless, who was wretched and He came forth in the Person of the Lord Jesus Christ. He came forth as the One who cared, as the One who was worthy, as the One who was able. In Isaiah 59:17, He came forth as the Great Hero of mercy, as the Deliverer of the enslaved, as the Friend of the perishing, mighty to save, competent to heal, and ready to emancipate regardless of a person's guilt or condition.

See Him . . . Pulling a man out of a tree.
Pulling a man out of the water.
Pulling a man out of a coffin.
Pulling a man out of a grave.
Pulling a man out of the door of hell.
Pulling a man out of despair.
Pulling a man out of sin.
Pulling a man out of his misery.

Hear Him . . Speaking a man out of deafness.
Speaking a man out of dumbness.
Speaking a man out of blindness.
Speaking a man out of lameness.
Speaking a man out of sinfulness.
Speaking a man out of deadness.
Speaking a man out of darkness.

Sitting here at my desk at 12:19 a.m., I hear the words, He Came to Me.

I was limping and dragging when He came to me.
I was weary and hurting when He came to me.
I was angry and disappointed when He came to me.
I was downtrodden and exploited when He came to me.
I was sick and afflicted when He came to me.
I was restless and listless when He came to me.
I was bereaved, grieved, and heavy-ladened when He came to me.

Conclusion

God, in Jesus Christ, came to this earth as man.
He came by way of a woman.
He grew up in the cottage of Nazareth.
He ate at the table of publicans and sinners.
He slept in a ship on the water.
He wept at the grave of Lazarus.
He shuddered on the ground in Gethsemane.
He bled on the cross of Calvary.
He arose from the dark tomb.
He clothed Himself in humanity.
He identified Himself with man.
He was wounded in our sorrow to give us joy.
He was clouded in our darkness to give us light.
He was pierced in our coldness to give us warmth.
He was crucified in our death to give us life – Life Eternal!

Hebrews 2:17 *"Wherefore in all things it behoved him to be made like unto his brethren, that he might be a merciful and faithful high priest in things pertaining to God, to make reconciliation for the sins of the people."*

Chapter 5

Help Me!

Isaiah 63:5 *"And I looked, and there was none to help; and I wondered that there was none to uphold."*

This verse, in its proper setting, seems to express the idea that there would be no man to bring deliverance to Judah. As I read these words, I hear the cry of today . . . Help Me!

The cry is heard in the social world, Help Me!
The cry is heard in the economic world, Help Me!
The cry is heard in the physical world, Help Me!
The cry is heard in the spiritual world, Help Me!

The cry comes from the youth who feel that life is a mistake. The cry is amplified, Please Help Me! I read in a "Dear Abby" article years ago as a teenager wrote about her devastated life, Please Help Me!

The cry comes from parents who feel that life is a blunder, Please Help Me!
The cry comes from the elderly who feel that life is a regret, Please Help Me!
The cry is heard among the diseased and afflicted, Please Help Me!
The cry is heard among the lost and dying, Please Help Me!
The cry is heard among the grieved and bereaved, Please Help Me!

The cry is heard among the deprived and exploited,
Please Help Me!
The cry is heard among the distraught and distressed,
Please Help Me!

This cry, Please Help Me!, is seen in people's actions.
This cry, Please Help Me!, is seen in people's expressions.

The Psalmist of old knew where Help was!!! He said,
"I will lift up mine eyes unto the hills, from whence cometh my help. ²My help cometh from the LORD, which made heaven and earth." Psalm 121:1-2.

"In my distress I called upon the LORD, and cried unto my God: he heard my voice out of his temple, and my cry came before him, even into his ears. ⁹He bowed the heavens also, and came down: and darkness was under his feet."
Psalms 18:6, 9.

Glory!
HE sits on the circle of the earth.
HE rides on the wings of the wind.
HE walks on the waves of the sea.
HE is our Help!!!

Astronomers are looking through telescopes, investigating the solar system, but are not giving us a sure direction for survival.

Chemists are looking into test tubes, making great advancements, but are not giving us a solution to many of our problems.

Geologists are looking into the ages of the past, digging into fossilized rocks, and discovering the graves of once-living creatures, but are not telling us how to live or die.

Ecologists are looking into every phase of our environment, probing and analyzing, but are not providing us an escape from this ole polluted world.

Psalm 60:11 *"Give us help from trouble: for vain is the help of man."*

Isaiah 63:5 *"And I looked, and there was none to help."*

Psalm 33:20 *"He is **our help** and **our** shield."*

Psalm 46:1 *"**God is our** refuge and strength, a very present **help** in trouble."*

Psalm 109:26 *"**Help me**, O LORD my God."*

Psalm 124:8 *"**Our help is in the name of the LORD**, who made heaven and earth."*

Part II

Sermons for Special Occasions

Chapter 6

Church Celebration Time

We are here today to celebrate the Fort Mill Church of God, Fort Mill, South Carolina. On September 27, 1931, nineteen believers stepped forth to be declared the Fort Mill Church of God. Sister Ida Perry was the only one that I remember. (Thank you, David Ward, Jr., for this information.)

Sometime after June 5, 1936, (my birth time), I started an acquaintance with many of the church folk, including my Daddy and Mother. The little excited group had church in a small building (across the tracks) behind Culp's Ice House. I saw this little building just this morning while driving around.

Odell Walker put his name on the line when he purchased this property on Academy Street and turned it over to the Church of God. What a campus now! I well remember the building on the mountain and the Episcopal or Catholic church building that was moved and placed beside the sanctuary.

Regardless of the strange practical teachings, the attitude of the small town and some of the town citizens, and being started on the other side of the tracks, the Fort Mill Church has become the strongest church in town and one of the strongest in the denomination. I am proud to be a product of the Fort Mill Church of God.

Let's look at a setting in Genesis 28 after Jacob and his mother had deceitfully taken the family birthright from Esau.

Jacob was sent away to escape the fury of Esau. His first night away from home is recorded here in Genesis 28:10-11, *"And Jacob went out from Beersheba, and went toward Haran. ¹¹ And he lighted upon a certain place, and tarried there all night, because the sun was set; and he took of the stones of that place, and put them for his pillows, and lay down in that place to sleep."*

He took stones and made pillows. The ground was his couch/bed. The canopy of the sky his covering. The stars in the heaven his company.

Oh, but what an Experience!

- o He saw a ladder that connected Heaven and Earth.
- o He saw angels, the spiritual host of God, ascending and descending.
- o He saw the Lord at the top of the ladder.
- o He heard the voice of God, comforting, consoling, inspiring, and supporting.
- o He, Jacob, exclaimed, "This is the House of God."

He did church things – He rose up early! He made an altar. He poured oil on the altar (the Holy Spirit). He vowed a vow: He promised to pay the tithe (some of our parents endorsed their weekly paychecks and gave them to this church). Let's celebrate them! He then testified. He proclaimed the Lord to be his God!

Now, let's look at Verse 17, *"And he was afraid, and said, How dreadful is this place! this is none other but the house of God, and this is the gate of heaven."*

- This is a dreadful place.
- This is the house of God.
- This is the gate of Heaven.

Now, let's look at Genesis 29:1, *"Then Jacob went on his journey, and came into the land of the people of the east."* Then, <u>Then</u>, Jacob went on his journey. We are on our journey and I say, 'Thank God for the Church.' Thank God for the Fort Mill Church of God.

You can call the church by whatever name or reference you desire: The House of God, The Sanctuary of the Lord, the Temple of Jehovah, the Body of Christ, A Living Spiritual Organism, or A Called-Out Assembly.

But today, we celebrate the Fort Mill Church of God as we journey. Listen, we are on a journey, an untried journey, but, we have the Church. There is much along the way to try us, to vex us, to disturb us, to discourage us, to overwhelm us, to destroy us. But Praise God! We have the Church. Let's Celebrate!

Consider our condition when we found the Church or when the Church rescued us:
Some of us were limping and dragging.
Some of us were weary and hurting.
Some of us were angry and disappointed.
Some of us were downtrodden and exploited.
Some of us were sick and afflicted.
Some of us were bereaved and heavy-ladened.

Like the Psalmist records in Psalm 73:2-3: *'We were disturbed and confused. Our feet were almost gone, our steps had well nigh slipped. We were envious at the foolish who seemingly were having a good time in life."*

We could not reason it out. We could not understand it. We could not accept what was happening. Until . . . we went into the sanctuary of the Lord. Then it all cleared up. Now we are in the Church – Let's Celebrate! Let's raise our hands in adoration to the Lord. Let's lift our voices in praise to the Lord. Hallelujah!

> We are in Church:
> Let us voice our fears
> Let us acknowledge our faith
> Let us confess our faults
> Let us exercise our freedom in worship.
> Let tears fall
> Let's reclaim our hope
> Let the Lord restore our joy in this time of celebration.

> This is the time and place:
> To pour out your soul
> To proclaim your hope
> To acknowledge your faith.
> Let your heart be comforted
> Let your soul be cheered
> Let your spirit be exuberated
> Let your mind be refreshed.

Hear Psalm 77:13 *"Thy way, O God, is in the sanctuary."* God can do His business anywhere, even on the backside of the desert.

Psalm 122:1 *"I was glad when they said unto me, Let us go into the house of the LORD."*

Psalm 42:4 *"I went with them to the house of God, with the voice of joy and praise, with a multitude that kept holyday."*

Psalm 84:10 *"For a day in thy courts is better than a thousand. I had rather be a doorkeeper in the house of my God, than to dwell in the tents of wickedness."*

We have no idea about future happenings: burdens to bear, afflictions to suffer, trials to endure, enemies to fight, temptations to encounter, and death to face. The child of God does not always live in flowery beds of ease. There is a devil to fight, there is a world to face, and there is the flesh to engage.

So, let us celebrate today and be ready, be prepared for whatever may come tomorrow.

Chapter 7

Pastor Appreciation

In the book of Ephesians, Chapter 4, it seems that our resurrected Lord was setting in order the New Testament church, as Paul writes in Verse 11: *"And he gave some, apostles; and some, prophets; and some, evangelists; and some, pastors and teachers;* ¹²*For the perfecting of the saints, for the work of the ministry, for the edifying of the body of Christ."* The *"body of Christ"* refers to the Church.

"And some, Pastors." As a Pastor, for most of the past 65 years, I feel that I have been an apostle, a prophet, an evangelist, and a teacher. No doubt your Pastor has felt the same. We could add a few more things to the list: advocate, peacemaker, storm calmer, custodian, plumber, carpenter, cook, etc.

But let's zero in on *"and some, Pastors."*

The original meaning of the word, Pastor, was shepherd, and in this sense, it is sometimes used in the Bible. The responsibility of the eastern Shepherd was to protect and feed the sheep. From this, we derive the thought that a Pastor is a spiritual leader in charge of a church – to protect the flock and to feed them – to feed their souls spiritually.

The Lord issued some strong words against unfaithful Pastors in the Old Testament. Jeremiah 2:8 shows that the Lord takes note of Pastors, *". . . the pastors also transgressed against me. . ."*

When God called Israel and Judah to repent, He promised them true Pastors. Jeremiah 3:15, *"And I will give you pastors according to mine heart, which shall feed you with knowledge and understanding."*

Hear the sad words that are recorded in Jeremiah 10:21, *"For the pastors are become brutish, and have not sought the LORD: therefore they shall not prosper, and all their flocks shall be scattered."* And in Jeremiah 12:10, *"Many pastors have destroyed my vineyard, they have trodden my portion under foot, they have made my pleasant portion a desolate wilderness."*

Hear Jeremiah 23:1-4, *"Woe be unto the pastors that destroy and scatter the sheep of my pasture! saith the LORD. 2 Therefore thus saith the LORD God of Israel against the pastors that feed my people; Ye have scattered my flock, and driven them away, and have not visited them: behold, I will visit upon you the evil of your doings, saith the LORD. 3 And I will gather the remnant of my flock out of all countries whither I have driven them, and will bring them again to their folds; and they shall be fruitful and increase. 4 And I will set up shepherds over them which shall feed them: and they shall fear no more, nor be dismayed, neither shall they be lacking, saith the LORD."*

And I say, "Praise the Lord for Pastors like 'Pastor Edgar Foster'!

Do you understand what it takes to have a church? I am qualified to tell you what it takes to start a church and what it takes to keep on going. It takes:

- Three P's - People, Place, and Preacher (Pastor)
- Three M's - Mission (Purpose), Music, and Money (Means)
- Three G's - Grit, Grace, and Grind

The person that leads all of this, is, the Pastor. A successful Pastor must have some of the same characteristics as Caleb, as recorded in the Book of Numbers, Chapter 14, *"The words of the Lord,"* *"my servant Caleb,"* and *"hath followed me fully."*   Caleb was one of the twelve men who were sent by Moses to check out the land that the Lord would give His children, the children of Israel.

Ten men returned with a fearful report that dismayed and disturbed the people, the congregation of Israel. They lifted up their voices, they cried out, they wept all night – they murmured exceedingly!

Numbers 13:30, *"And Caleb stilled the people before Moses."* What ability! 'Like Caleb' means:

- The law of God was in his heart.
- The spirit of God was in his life.
- He stood firm, he held fast, he did not waver.
- He was devout, earnest, and sincere.
- He was dedicated and faithful – all the way.
- He was diligent, persevering, and continuing.
- He was a man of God!

Like Caleb, Edgar Foster is a man of God, 'a servant of the Lord.' Like Caleb, I feel Pastor Edgar Foster realizes that there is no rest without a journey, that there is no reward without labor, and that there is no victory without warfare.

I feel that your pastor will run til he reaches the goal. That he will fight til the crown is gained. That he will persevere til the promise is obtained. That he will continue til the Lord declares, "Well done! You have fought a good fight. Welcome Home!" Until that time comes, I feel Pastor Edgar Foster will fulfill his leadership with his flock who is on a journey.

On this Journey –

- o There may be rivers to cross
- o Wilderness to encounter
- o Mountains to climb
- o Walled cities to take
- o Giants to subdue, put down
- o Enemies to fight
- o Obstacles to overcome
- o Temptations to allure
- o Afflictions to engulf
- o Trials to engage
- o Shadows to frighten
- o Death to face

I believe Pastor Foster will be in front of his flock, crying out, *"Thanks be to God, which giveth us the victory through our Lord Jesus Christ. Therefore, my beloved brethren, be ye stedfast, unmoveable, always abounding in the work of the Lord, forasmuch as ye know that your labour is not in vain in the Lord."* 1 Corinthians 15:57-58.

Oh, and what about the Pastor's wife?

The Pastor's Wife:

- o A Pastor's calling becomes her calling.
- o A Pastor's place of ministry becomes her place of ministry.
- o A Pastor's living accommodations become her place accommodation (regardless of colors).
- o A Pastor's type of ministry becomes her type of ministry.
- o A Pastor's financial compensation becomes her financial compensation.
- o A Pastor's criticism becomes her criticism and heartache.

In Conclusion

- o A good Church and a good Pastor just go together.
- o A good Church can help to make a good Pastor.
- o You may be limping and dragging today, but you have a Church and a Pastor.
- o You may be weary and hurting today, but Praise the Lord, you have a Church and a Pastor.
- o You may be angry and disappointed today, but you have a Church and a Pastor.
- o You may be sick and afflicted today, but you have a Church and a Pastor.
- o You may be bereaved and heavy-laden today, but you have a Church and a Pastor.

A real Pastor understands . . . So . . .
>Let your soul be cheered today, right now!
>Let your spirit be exuberated today,
>Let your mind be refreshed today.

Praise God for a Church and a Pastor!
Praise God for a Good Church and a Good Pastor!

Chapter 8

Mother's Day Message

Mother's Day received national recognition on May 8, 1914 – to be observed annually on the second Sunday of May. It is with Love, Joy, and Appreciation that we honor our mothers today.

Hear our Scripture: 2 Kings 4:18-19 *"And when the child was grown, it fell on a day, that he went out to his father to the reapers. [19] And he said unto his father, My head, my head. And he said to a lad, Carry him to his mother."*

There are times when the wheels of life run smoothly and one day is like another. Then again, there are times when changes come as quickly as lightning, and years of joy and/or sorrow may be concentrated in a single day. So it was with the Shunammite household of 2 Kings, Chapter 4. The man and woman in this setting followed the regular routine of life for many years. That is until the prophet (Elisha) came into their lives.

The couple of our story showed the Prophet so much kindness that he stopped at their home often. Now, Elisha wanted to give some kind of remuneration for their often-expressed hospitality. Verse 10 states they made him a little chamber – a bed, a table, a lamp, a stool, and a candlestick.

He questioned the lady of the house as to what he could do in return for their continual kindness to him. Elisha reminded her of such kindness saying in Verse 13, *"Behold, thou hast been careful for us with all this care; what is to be done for thee? wouldest thou be spoken for to the king, or to the captain of the host?"* (She did not care for any recognition or honor).

So, Elisha spoke to his servant and said, "What can we do for her?" Verse 14, *"She has no son."* Now that Scripture may not seem desperate to some women, but the Hebrews were anxious to have children, especially to have a son.

The Prophet called her and declared in Verse 16, *"According to the time of life, thou shalt embrace a son."* Verse 17 gives the fulfillment, *"And the woman conceived, and bare a son at that season that Elisha had said unto her, according to the time of life."*

The boy became the joy of his mother and the pride of his father.   But who knows what a day may bring forth? Proverbs 27:1, *"For thou knowest not what a day may bring forth."*   A day can begin with Joy and end in Sorrow.
- From Happiness – To Sadness
- From Health – To Affliction
- From Laughter – To Tears
- From Life – to Death
- From Dreams – to Nightmare

That brings us to our Scripture and subject – *"Carry him to his mother."*
- The father was not shunning his responsibility.
- The father was not too busy.
- The father was not taking his son's cry lightly.

The father knew where comfort and care could be found for his son - *"Carry him to his mother."* It was the instinct of the father's heart. He knew that no one would give him the care and attention like the son's mother would give. He knew that his mother would do the right thing, the right action, and whatever was needed!

Listen! A child may be hurt, others may make light of it, but not his mother.

A child may be weary (slow) of learning, while others are fast and impatient, but the mother is tender and forbearing.

A child may be stricken with sickness or affliction while others continue their ordinary routine of life.

But, the mother serves as a refuge – laying aside all personal comforts, forgetting time, and toiling continually.

A son or daughter may have committed a terrible act of sin. While others are severe and harsh, the mother is merciful and understanding.

A son or daughter may be rejected and dejected by others, but not by mother! It is no wonder the father said, *"Carry him to his mother."*

In conclusion, it is sad to read the rest of the story, 2 Kings 4:20, *"And when he had taken him, and brought him to his mother, he sat on her knees till noon, and then died.*

Verse 20: She went after the man of God.

Verse 23: Her husband seemingly tried to keep her from going after the preacher. *"And he said, Wherefore wilt thou go to him to day? it is neither new moon, nor sabbath. And she said, It shall be well."*

Verse 24: *"Then she saddled an ass."*

Verse 25: The prophet saw her coming.

Verse 27: *"And when she came to the man of God to the hill, she caught him by the feet."*

Verse 28: Then, *"she said, Did I desire a son of my lord? did I not say, Do not deceive me?"*

Verse 30-37: *"And the mother of the child said, As the LORD liveth, and as thy soul liveth, I will not leave thee. And he arose, and followed her. 31 And Gehazi passed on before them, and laid the staff upon the face of the child; but there was neither voice, nor hearing. Wherefore he went again to meet him, and told him, saying, The child is not awaked. 32 And when Elisha was come into the house, behold, the child was dead, and laid upon his bed. 33 He went in therefore, and shut the door upon them twain, and prayed unto the LORD. 34 And he went up, and lay upon the child, and put his mouth upon his mouth, and his eyes upon his eyes, and his hands upon his hands: and he stretched himself upon the child; and the flesh of the child waxed warm. 35 Then he returned, and walked in the house to and fro; and went up, and stretched himself upon him: and the child sneezed seven times, and the child opened his eyes. 36 And he called Gehazi, and said, Call this Shunammite. So he called her. And when she was come in unto him, he said . . .*

> *Take up thy son. 37 Then she went in, and fell at his feet, and bowed herself to the ground, and took up her son, and went out."*

It is time to shout right here, right now on Mother's Day!

Phyllis and I thank the Lord for our mothers, Irene Menke and Lily Mae Johnson.

Chapter 9

Becoming A Widow

A marriage precedes widowhood. A ceremony, called a wedding ceremony, binds together a man and a woman as husband and wife. The words "I Do" bind them together. The wedding rings signify to all their union as husband and wife. All of this occurs within a few minutes, and the officiating minister declares that the couple is husband and wife.

For a woman to become a widow takes only a moment. A woman does not become a widow by the declaration of a minister or a government official. A woman becomes a widow without the exchanging of rings. A woman becomes a widow without saying the marriage vows and/or the two simple words, "I Do." A woman becomes a widow without any type of ceremony.

A woman becomes a widow when her husband breathes his last breath. This dawned on me when I stood by the bedside of my friend, Ralph Raines. When he drew his last breath, Helen became a widow. Immediately, at that moment, her uncertainties began - not the next day, not even the next hour, but that very moment, immediately!

She, as a widow, had to assume responsibilities that were often overwhelming. What a list! The mortuary, the funeral service, family affairs, family finance, and children.

Sometimes she is in the same situation as the widow of 2 Kings 4:1-2 whose two sons were bondmen.

41

Sometimes she is a pastor's wife. The church pastor dies and within a few weeks, she must vacate the parsonage. Often a pastor's wife who becomes a widow must find employment; she must deal with children and their schools.

Sometimes she may be 36 years old with three children to raise, ages from 2 to 11 years.

She, as a widow, may find herself as the widow of 1 Kings 17 that had only enough food for one more meal.

Pastor Johnson took care of one such situation when he fell in love with Phyllis Walls. You can read about it in his book, "Taking A Chance With God." Phyllis was not destitute. She owned her house and vehicle, and she had no mortgages to face, but she was only 36 years of age and had three children to raise.

Take a look in the Old Testament and see how the Lord took care of widows:

    1 Kings 17
    2 Kings 4
    2 Kings 8

Now hear James 1:27, *"Pure religion and undefiled before God and the Father is this, To visit the fatherless and widows in their affliction, and to keep himself unspotted from the world."*

Chapter 10

The Palm Tree

(Senior Adult Emphasis)

I used this thought and this Scripture forty years ago. I have no idea where or when I obtained this information.

Psalm 92:12-15, *"The righteous shall flourish like the palm tree: he shall grow like a cedar in Lebanon.*
13 Those that be planted in the house of the LORD shall flourish in the courts of our God.
14 They shall still bring forth fruit in old age; they shall be fat and flourishing;
15 To shew that the LORD is upright: he is my rock, and there is no unrighteousness in him."

The Palm Tree flourishes without intermission. It flourishes despite hindrances while other trees wither and die. Excessive dryness does not arrest it; copious rains do not overstimulate it; the summer's most fierce heat doesn't wither it; and, the strongest wind doesn't bend it.

Remove its back, and it still flourishes. Girdle it, and it still flourishes. In spite of hindrances or conditions, it still flourishes.

The Palm Tree grows from one century and into the next century. It may be slow in growth, but it is sure and steady, it keeps growing. As years pass by, it is more in height, more in bulk, and more in strength. Men have tried unsuccessfully to hinder its straightness by hanging heavy weights upon it, but it continues to grow upward.

The Palm Tree is most useful. Wine is made from the sap. The seeds are made into food for camels. The fibers of the leaf stem are woven into ropes. The tall trunk is valuable for timber. Even its leaves are made into many different articles. Its fruit is a daily food for many. The palm tree is one of the most useful trees on planet Earth.

The Bible declares that *"the righteous shall flourish like the palm tree."* I have a thought, 'If you were a tree, what kind of a tree would you like to be? Would it be a palm tree?' – advancing from grace to grace, advancing from strength to strength, advancing from glory to glory?

Flourishing. Yes, how wonderful! Flourishing amidst the infirmities of a decaying nature. The eyes may grow dim, the voice weak, the hair silver, and the steps slow, but flourishing, greater and sweeter as the days go by. There are some reasons (secrets) for the flourishing of a palm tree.
- Its roots extend far and deep into the earth extending themselves until they find a spring or river.
- Its life is in the heart, not in the bark.
- Its success is achieved by the unfolding of its inner life.

Psalm 1:3 *"And he* (the righteous) *shall be like a tree planted by the rivers of water, that bringeth forth his fruit in his season; his leaf also shall not wither; and whatsoever he doeth shall prosper."*

2 Corinthians 4:16 *"But the outward man perish, yet the inward man is renewed day by day."*

Psalm 84:7 *"They (the righteous) go from strength to strength."* Hear again . . . They, the Palm Tree, shall bring forth fruit in old age! That reminds me of the song – 'It gets sweeter as the days go by.'

Chapter 11

Crucify Him

Luke 23:21 *"They cried, saying, Crucify him, crucify him."*

The mob did not consider who Jesus was, so they cried, "Crucify Him, Crucify Him!" They did not consider that Jesus, according to John 1:29 was *"the Lamb of God, which taketh away the sin of the world."*

They did not consider the witness, written in John 1:34: *"And I saw, and bare record that this is the Son of God."*

They did not consider, according to Matthew 3:17, the voice from heaven, saying, *"This is my beloved son, in whom I am well please."*

They did not consider, according to Matthew 16:16, the glorious declaration, *"Thou art the Christ, the Son of the living God."*

They refused to consider that Jesus was the Word of God, the Son of God, the Chosen of God, the Gift of God, and the Power of God.

They did not accept the fact that He was the Word of God, John 1:1-4, *"In the beginning was the Word, and the Word was with God, and the Word was God. 2 The same was in the beginning with God. 3 All things were made by him; and without him was not any thing made that was made. 4 In him was life; and the life was the light of men."*

The mob repudiated the fact that Jesus was:
       God in thought
       God in image
       God in grace
       God in mercy
       God in truth.
So they cried, Crucify Him!

They could not see that He was:
       The Rose of Sharon
       The Lily of the Valley
       The Balm of Gilead.
So they cried, Crucify Him!

They could not see that He was:
       The Star of Astronomy
       The Rock of Geology
       The Lion of Judah!
So they cried, Crucify Him!

They could not see that He was:
       The Lamb of God
       The Son of God
       The Lord of Lords
       The King of Kings
       The Bright and Morning Star.
So they cried, Crucify Him!

They refused to be a witness to His works. And oh, what works!!

When Jesus met leprous men, He cleansed them.
When Jesus met crippled men, He made them walk.

When Jesus met dumb men, He made them talk.
When Jesus met deaf men, He made them hear.
When Jesus met outcast men, He restored them.
When Jesus met critics, He confounded them.
When Jesus met a devil, He subdued it.
When Jesus met a funeral procession, He broke it up.
When Jesus entered a cemetery, He disturbed it.
When Jesus faced a hungry crowd, He fed them.

Yet, the mob cried, Crucify Him!

They wanted Him to suffer.
They wanted Him to face shame.
They wanted Him to be treated as a criminal.
They wanted Him to be disgraced.
They wanted Him to be dishonored.

The cross meant the greatest horror, the greatest shame, the greatest pain, the greatest indecency, so they cried, Crucify Him! According to Luke 23:14-24, Pilate tried to reason with the mob, but his attempt to reason with them did not change their minds.

According to Matthew 27:19, Pilate's wife spoke out saying, *"Have thou nothing to do with that just man: for I have suffered many things this day in a dream because of him."* Her distress over the situation did not change anyone's mind.

According to Luke 23:27, *"And there followed him a great company of people, and of women, which also bewailed and lamented him."* This bewailing and lamenting by this group following him made no difference. The cry continued, Crucify Him, Crucify Him!

So, they crucified Him!   Earth has no darker sin. History has no blacker page.   Humanity has no fouler spot than the ignominious death of Jesus Christ, our Lord.

No wonder the heavens went black.
No wonder the sun withdrew its light.
No wonder the graves burst open.
No wonder the earth reeled and rocked.
No wonder the veil of the Temple rent in twain from the top to the bottom.

The curtain came down at Calvary.   The mob was satisfied.   Jesus Christ, our Lord, was crucified!

He is dead.

John 19:30 tells us that He was dead as He dropped His head on a pulseless breast and shouted, '*It is finished,*' and gave up the ghost.

The curious crowd said - He is dead.
The callous Roman soldiers said - He is dead.
The prating Pharisees said – He is dead.
Mary, His heartbroken Mother said – He is dead.
His disciples, stunned with disbelief, said – He is dead.
The cry ceased! He was crucified!

All four Gospel writers included this story in their books called by their names: Matthew, Mark, Luke, and John.

Chapter 12

A Thorn

2 Corinthians 12:7-10: *"And lest I should be exalted above measure through the abundance of the revelations, there was given to me a thorn in the flesh, the messenger of Satan to buffet me, lest I should be exalted above measure. 8 For this thing I besought the Lord thrice, that it might depart from me. 9 And he said unto me, My grace is sufficient for thee: for my strength is made perfect in weakness. Most gladly therefore will I rather glory in my infirmities, that the power of Christ may rest upon me. 10 Therefore I take pleasure in infirmities, in reproaches, in necessities, in persecutions, in distresses for Christ's sake: for when I am weak, then am I strong."*

Paul had a problem – a thorn in the flesh. Because of Galatians 4:13-15, some think his thorn was an affliction of the eyes:

"Ye know how through infirmity of the flesh I preached the gospel unto you at the first. 14 And my temptation which was in my flesh ye despised not, nor rejected; but received me as an angel of God, even as Christ Jesus. 15 Where is then the blessedness ye spake of? for I bear you record, that, if it had been possible, ye would have plucked out your own eyes, and have given them to me."

Paul described this affliction as a *"thorn in the flesh - a messenger of Satan to buffet me,"* 2 Corinthians 12:7. *"Buffet"* means 'a blow.' It seems that his problem was a physical malady. It was troublesome, disturbing, and always present. His problem caused bodily weakness and produced a repulsive appearance. The problem affected him physically and emotionally.

The apostle's thorn is not described precisely in the Scriptures, so his consolations may avail for all of us with any kind of thorn. A thorn could be physical, emotional, psychological, financial, or otherwise. A thorn in the flesh could be anything that continually hinders, that continually bothers, that continually interrupts.

HOW GOD RESPONDS

God responded when Paul sought the Lord concerning his painful problem. Paul prayed until God heard him. Like others, he sought God and the Lord responded favorably to him.

The psalmist sought the Lord. *"In my distress I called upon the LORD,"* he remembered, *"and cried out to my God"* (Psalm 18:6). God's response is recorded in Verses 16-19: *"He sent from above, he took me, he drew me out of many waters. 17 He delivered me from my strong enemy, and from them which hated me: for they were too strong for me. 18 They prevented me in the day of my calamity: but the LORD was my stay. 19 He brought me forth also into a large place; he delivered me, because he delighted in me."*

Luke, Chapter 18:40-43, records the story of the blind man and God's response: *"And Jesus stood, and commanded him to be brought unto him: and when he was come near, he asked him, 41 Saying, What wilt thou that I shall do unto thee? And he said, Lord, that I may receive my sight.*

42 And Jesus said unto him, Receive thy sight: thy faith hath saved thee. 43 And immediately he received his sight, and followed him, glorifying God: and all the people, when they saw it, gave praise unto God."

Paul was a praying man. He believed in the power of prayer!
- In 1 Corinthians 14, he prayed in the spirit and in tongues.
- In 1 Thessalonians 5:25, he asked for prayer.
- In 2 Thessalonians 3:1, he petitioned for prayer.
- In 1 Timothy 2:8, he encouraged prayer.
- In Acts 16:25, he prayed before he sang in the Philippian jail.

EXCUSES PAUL DID NOT MAKE

Thus accustomed to praying, Paul prayed three times for the *"thorn in the flesh"* to be taken away. But God said, *"No."* He could have appealed to Jesus' own words:
"And whatsoever ye shall ask in my name, that will I do, that the Father may be glorified in the Son. 14 If ye shall ask any thing in my name, I will do it." John 14:13,14.
"If ye abide in me, and my words abide in you, ye shall ask what ye will, and it shall be done unto you." John 15:7.

He could have appealed to his own experiences when God answered prayer: (Paul) *"Said with a loud voice, Stand upright on thy feet. And* (the man crippled from his mother's womb) *he leaped and walked."* Acts 14:10.

He could have appealed to the miracle when he was stoned and left for dead at Lystra: Acts 14:19-20. *"And there came thither certain Jews from Antioch and Iconium, who persuaded the people, and, having stoned Paul, drew him out of the city, supposing he had been dead. 20 Howbeit, as the disciples stood round about him, he rose up, and came into the city: and the next day he departed with Barnabas to Derbe."*

Paul could have appealed to his own sacrifice, faithfulness, and service to Christ: 2 Corinthians 11:23-28. *"Are they ministers of Christ? (I speak as a fool) I am more; in labours more abundant, in stripes above measure, in prisons more frequent, in deaths oft. 24 Of the Jews five times received I forty stripes save one. 25 Thrice was I beaten with rods, once was I stoned, thrice I suffered shipwreck, a night and a day I have been in the deep; 26 In journeyings often, in perils of waters, in perils of robbers, in perils by mine own countrymen, in perils by the heathen, in perils in the city, in perils in the wilderness, in perils in the sea, in perils among false brethren; 27 In weariness and painfulness, in watchings often, in hunger and thirst, in fastings often, in cold and nakedness. 28 Beside those things that are without, that which cometh upon me daily, the care of all the churches."*

HOW OTHERS REACTED TO GOD'S NO

Paul was not the first person to face this dilemma. Others faced *'NO'* answers from God, too. How did they react? When the Babylonians threatened to throw three Hebrew boys into a fiery furnace that was heated seven times hotter than usual, these Biblical heroes were ready with an answer . . . even if God said *NO!*

Daniel 3:16-18, *"Shadrach, Meshach, and Abednego, answered and said to the king, O Nebuchadnezzar, we are not careful to answer thee in this matter. 17 If it be so, our God whom we serve is able to deliver us from the burning fiery furnace, and he will deliver us out of thine hand, O king. 18 But if not, be it known unto thee, O king, that we will not serve thy gods, nor worship the golden image which thou hast set up."*

Why does God say *NO?* He has a plan, a purpose, and a will! 1 John 5:14-15, *"And this is the confidence that we have in him, that, if we ask any thing according to his will, he heareth us: 15 And if we know that he hear us, whatsoever we ask, we know that we have the petitions that we desired of him."*

What was Jesus' reaction when God the Father said *NO!*

Matthew 26:36-46, *"Then cometh Jesus with them unto a place called Gethsemane, and saith unto the disciples, Sit ye here, while I go and pray yonder. 37 And he took with him Peter and the two sons of Zebedee, and began to be sorrowful and very heavy. 38 Then saith he unto them, My soul is exceeding sorrowful, even unto death: tarry ye here, and watch with me.*

39 And he went a little further, and fell on his face, and prayed, saying, O my Father, if it be possible, let this cup pass from me: nevertheless not as I will, but as thou wilt. 40 And he cometh unto the disciples, and findeth them asleep, and saith unto Peter, What, could ye not watch with me one hour? 41 Watch and pray, that ye enter not into temptation: the spirit indeed is willing, but the flesh is weak.

42 He went away again the second time, and prayed, saying, O my Father, if this cup may not pass away from me, except I drink it, thy will be done. *43 And he came and found them asleep again: for their eyes were heavy.*

44 And he left them, and went away again, and prayed the third time, saying the same words. 45 Then cometh he to his disciples, and saith unto them, Sleep on now, and take your rest: behold, the hour is at hand, and the Son of man is betrayed into the hands of sinners. 46 Rise, let us be going: behold, he is at hand that doth betray me."

Jesus accepted the *NO* answer and said, *"Nevertheless, not as I will, but as You will."* He refused to be angry, disappointed, or disturbed.

What was Paul's reaction to God's saying NO? It is penned so beautifully in the *Living Bible,* 2 Corinthians 12:8-10:

"Three different times I begged God to make me well again. Each time he said, 'No. But I am with you; that is all you need. My power shows up best in weak people.' Now I am glad to boast about how weak I am; I am glad to be a living demonstration of Christ's power, instead of showing off my own power and abilities. Since I know it is all for Christ's good, I am quite happy about 'the thorn' and about insults and hardships, persecutions, and difficulties; for when I am weak, then I am strong – the less I have, the more I depend on him."

Paul accepted the *NO* answer by the grace of God, and declared he would . . .
- *live with it* . . . by the grace of God
- *bear it* . . . by the grace of God
- *adjust to it* . . . by the grace of God
- *glory in it* . . . by the grace of God
- *take pleasure in it* . . . by the grace of God.

CONCLUSION

Paul determined within himself that he would be strengthened by it. He knew that the power of Christ would be seen in it, and God would be magnified through it. Not only did Paul accept the *NO* answer, but he realized that God had a threefold divine purpose in saying *NO*:

1) To show the effectiveness of God's grace
2) To reveal the power of God in and through weakness
3) To promote humility (*"lest I should be exalted above measure by the abundance of the revelations,"* 2 Corinthians 12:7).

Physical weakness does not hinder the working of God. A weakness can cause greater productivity. Paul's response to the thorn in the flesh shows us how God turns Satan's best efforts to defeat us into usefulness for His glory. God can use what Satan intends for abuse. He can turn it into a blessing, a boost.

The key to victory is our response. Are you willing for the grace of God to be revealed in you? Are you willing for God's strength to be made perfect in your weakness? Are you willing to take pleasure in infirmities?

Are you aware that your "thorn in the flesh" may be the best thing that has ever happened to you? Your thorn may be your triumph! *Oh, but it's painful!* Sometimes it takes pain for us to pray. Sometimes it takes pain for us to produce. Sometimes it takes pain for us to be perfected! Sometimes it takes pain for us to recognize the power of God, and, to realize God's purpose in our lives.

Part III

Short Sermons

Chapter 13

Remember Who We Are

The 2017 British Open Golf Tournament was played in England. Golfers struggled. Conditions were adverse. The wind blew at all speeds in all directions. Short putts were missed. It was not a good day in Birkdale, England, for golfing. Nerves were on edge. World golfers were disgusted.

An announcer made a statement, "They need to remember who they are; they are world leaders."

When adversities are many,
> we need to remember "who we are."
When the way is difficult,
> we need to remember "who we are."
When burdens are heavy,
> we need to remember "who we are."
When the enemy is howling,
> we need to remember "who we are."
When the storm is raging,
> we need to remember "who we are."

When it seems that the end has come, that it is all over, we need to hear the Apostle Paul in Acts 27:23-24, *"For there stood by me this night the angel of God, whose I am, and whom I serve, 24 Saying, Fear not, Paul; thou must be brought before Caesar: and, lo, God hath given thee all them that sail with thee."*

Listen, Paul was outranked by the ship's captain. Paul was outmatched by the fury of nature (the storm was most destructive). Paul was outnumbered by the fellows that were on the boat – 275. However, Paul said in Verse 25, *"Wherefore, sirs, be of good cheer: for I believe God."*

Paul's faith in God turned the situation around. <u>His faith</u> in God outranked the captain of the ship, outmatched the fury of nature, outnumbered the 275 aboard, and it came to pass just as the Angel of the Lord said.

Read I John 3:2, *"Beloved, now are we the sons of God, and it doth not yet appear what we shall be: but we know that, when he shall appear, we shall be like him; for we shall see him as he is."*

Now, we are the children of God. When the journey is hard (difficult), <u>we need to remember "who we are."</u>

Chapter 14

Fear Not

Job 3:25 *"For the thing which I greatly <u>feared</u> is come upon me, and that which I was afraid of is come unto me."*

Fear is anxious anticipation of change, pain, and harm. Nothing affects man more than fear.

Fear can drench your sheets at night.
Fear can turn your dreams into nightmares.
Fear can cripple your vital forces.
Fear can sap your energy.
Fear can fray your nerves.
Fear can disturb your being.

When the Israelites stood before the Red Sea, Moses said, Exodus 14:13, *"Fear ye not, stand still, and see the salvation of the LORD, which he will shew to you to day."*

When Elijah confronted the widow of Zarephath and made his request for food, 1 Kings 17:13, he heard her confession, then he said, *"<u>Fear not</u>; go and do as thou hast said* (preparing the last meal for her son and herself)*: but make me thereof a little cake first."*

Jesus spoke "Fear not" through angels –
- To Joseph in Matthew, *"Fear not to take unto thee Mary thy wife."*
- To Zacharias in Luke 1:13, *"Fear not, Zacharias: for thy prayer is heard."*

- To Mary, *"Fear not, for thou hast found favour with God."*
- To the Shepherds in Luke 2:10, *"Fear not: for, behold, I bring you good tidings of great joy."*

Jesus to Simon – *"Fear not"* - Luke 5:10
Jesus to Jairus – *"Fear not"* - Luke 8:50
Jesus to His Flock – *"Fear not"* - Luke 12:32

Read about Paul's stormy voyage to Rome, Acts 27. Then get the message from the angel in Verse 24, *"Fear not, Paul; thou must be brought before Caesar: and, lo, God hath given thee all them that sail with thee."*

Fear can keep you from doing what God wants you to do.
Fear can keep you from being what God wants you to be.
Fear can keep you from going where God wants you to go.
Fear can keep you from giving what God wants you to give.
Fear can keep you from getting what God wants you to get.

Now hear Paul's response, Verse 25, *"Wherefore, sirs, be of good cheer: for I believe God."* Glory! Allow God to turn your fear into cheer!!!

Consider John's Patmos experience in Revelation, Chapter One. Then hear the voice of the Resurrected Lord in Verse 17, *"Fear not; I am the first and the last."*

Then Verse 18, *"I am he that liveth, and was dead; and, behold, I am alive for evermore, Amen; and have the keys of hell and of death."* Allow the Resurrected Lord to turn your fear into faith!!!

Chapter 15

Some Time

Some time we feel that there is no way out.
Some time we feel that the night will never end.
Some time we feel that the wounds will never heal.
Some time we feel that the burden will never be lifted.
Some time we feel that the problem will never be solved.
Some time we feel that the conflict will never be over.
Some time we feel that the guilt will never be gone.
Some time we feel that the battle will never be won.
Some time we feel that the devil will never leave us alone.

Read Matthew 4:1-11, *"Then was Jesus led up of the Spirit into the wilderness to be tempted of the devil. ² And when he had fasted forty days and forty nights, he was afterward an hungred. ³ And when the tempter came to him, he said, If thou be the Son of God, command that these stones be made bread.*

⁴ But he answered and said, It is written, Man shall not live by bread alone, but by every word that proceedeth out of the mouth of God.

⁵ Then the devil taketh him up into the holy city, and setteth him on a pinnacle of the temple, ⁶ And saith unto him, If thou be the Son of God, cast thyself down: for it is written, He shall give his angels charge concerning thee: and in their hands they shall bear thee up, lest at any time thou dash thy foot against a stone.

⁷ Jesus said unto him, It is written again, Thou shalt not tempt the Lord thy God.

8 Again, the devil taketh him up into an exceeding high mountain, and sheweth him all the kingdoms of the world, and the glory of them; 9 And saith unto him, All these things will I give thee, if thou wilt fall down and worship me.

10 Then saith Jesus unto him, Get thee hence, Satan: for it is written, Thou shalt worship the Lord thy God, and him only shalt thou serve.

11 Then the devil leaveth him, and, behold, angels came and ministered unto him."

Read Luke 4:1-13, *"And Jesus being full of the Holy Ghost returned from Jordan, and was led by the Spirit into the wilderness, 2 Being forty days tempted of the devil. And in those days he did eat nothing: and when they were ended, he afterward hungered. 3 And the devil said unto him, If thou be the Son of God, command this stone that it be made bread.*

4 And Jesus answered him, saying, It is written, That man shall not live by bread alone, but by every word of God.

5 And the devil, taking him up into an high mountain, shewed unto him all the kingdoms of the world in a moment of time. 6 And the devil said unto him, All this power will I give thee, and the glory of them: for that is delivered unto me; and to whomsoever I will I give it. 7 If thou therefore wilt worship me, all shall be thine.

8 And Jesus answered and said unto him, Get thee behind me, Satan: for it is written, Thou shalt worship the Lord thy God, and him only shalt thou serve.

9 And he brought him to Jerusalem, and set him on a pinnacle of the temple, and said unto him, If thou be the Son of God, cast thyself down from hence: 10 For it is written, He shall give his angels charge over thee, to keep thee: 11 And in their hands they shall bear thee up, lest at any time thou dash thy foot against a stone.

12 And Jesus answering said unto him, It is said, Thou shalt not tempt the Lord thy God.
13 And when the devil had ended all the temptation, he departed from him for a season."

My dad would say: He, Satan, will run out of seasons. According to Revelation, Chapter 20, Satan will be bound for a thousand years, then loosed for a season (his last season), Verse 2. Then in Verse 10, he will be cast into the lake of fire – his seasons will be ended.

Hear this Ole Bishop! The unpleasant situations that you face are only temporary. The valley through which you are walking is not permanent. The trials that you are encountering are only for a while. The devil that is causing most of your heartaches is seasonal. His seasons will end!!!

Some time we feel that the valley is too long.
Some time we feel that the mountain is too high.
Some time we feel that the sea is too wide.
Some time we feel that the road is too rough.
Some time we feel that the burden is too heavy.
Some time we feel that the problem is too severe.
Some time we feel that the cloud is too dark.

We become overwhelmed, overpowered, crushed, and buried. Oh, but when He speaks, you know the clouds will have to go, just because He loves us so.

And then we exclaim, *"Thanks be to God, which giveth us the victory through our Lord Jesus Christ."*! 1 Corinthians 15:57.

Chapter 16

Acknowledge Jesus

HE will take the fight out of the lions.
HE will take the heat out of the fire.
HE will take the sting out of the serpent.
HE will take the fear out of death.

Acknowledge Him. The sky will become clearer. The sun will become brighter. Heaven will become nearer.

Acknowledge Him. Situations will change. Problems will fade. Burdens will roll away.

Acknowledge Him. Sadness will be turned into joy. Darkness will be turned into light. Weakness will be turned into strength. Death will be turned into life.

Acknowledge Him. Sin will lose its dominion. Strongholds of Satan will crumble. Deliverance will come.

Have you gone as far as you can go?
    Then, acknowledge Him.
Have you employed all of your known means?
    Then, acknowledge Him.
Have you exhausted all of your available resources?
    Then, acknowledge Him.

Acknowledge Him as your Lord and Master and He will:

- Turn your fear to faith, and your
- Rags to riches, and your
- Poverty to plenty, and your
- Barrenness to bountifulness, and your
- Nothing to enough, and your
- Dreadfulness to delightfulness, and your
- Gloom to glory, and your
- Calamity to capital, and your
- Humility to honor, and your
- Anxiety to Assurance.

Chapter 17

He Knows

Remember the Lord knows everything about us, and He keeps a record. He is aware of our failures, our shortcomings, our misgivings, our actions, our reactions, our thoughts, intents, and faults.

He counts our steps, He bottles our tears, and He records our prayers. He remembers our good deeds, and He is aware of our bad deeds.

He knows the best about us. He knows the worse about us. He knows all of our secrets, good and bad.

He knows our unfilled desires, our unfinished hope, our unanswered longing, and our unexpressed fears.

He knows when despair is plaguing our souls. He knows when confusion is nagging our minds. He knows when devastation is wounding our spirit.

We need to remember who He is: when the furnace is heated seven times hotter than usual; when we face Goliath; when we face the Red Sea; and, when we face chilly Jordan.

We need to remember who the Lord is: when we approach the valley of the shadow of death; when the physician says, "I've done all I can;" when we have exhausted all of our means; and, when we have come to the end of our road.

Chapter 18

When the Lord Shows Up

Things happen when the Lord shows up! Luke, Chapter 8, verses 26-36, gives us an unusual story about what happens when Jesus shows up or when He comes upon a scene. In this story, a devil-possessed man was delivered of many devils, after which, the devils entered some swine, the swine ran violently down a steep place into the nearby lake, and they were choked.

When the Lord shows up, or could we say when the Lord takes over, things happen:

When the Lord shows up: mountains melt, seas separate, clouds disappear, and rain falls.

When the Lord shows up: furnaces cool, kings fall, enemies scatter, and satan bows and begs.

When the Lord shows up: darkness disappears, diseases flee, and leprosy vanishes.

When the Lord shows up: fire comes down, fear vanishes, and death surrenders its victims.

When the Lord shows up: lions take the lock-jaw, a cemetery becomes a salvation station, a death cell is converted into a sleeping quarter, and a barren land like Patmos is turned into a heavenly dreamland.

When Moses was on the backside of the desert, the Lord showed up and gave him courage and direction. When the Hebrew Boys were cast into the fiery furnace, the Lord showed up and reversed the thermostat that had been increased seven times hotter than usual.

When Daniel was thrown into the den with the lions as their evening meal, the Lord showed up and took away their appetite.

What is your situation? Expect the Lord to show up!

Chapter 19

Jesus, The Sweetest Name I Know

Speak it, Jesus.
Sing it, Jesus.
Shout it, Jesus.
Live it, Jesus.
Use it, Jesus.

Jesus, the sweetest Name I know,
The Name that calms our fears and bids our sorrows cease,
Jesus, 'tis music in our ears,
'Tis love, 'tis joy, 'tis peace.

May every star beam it, Jesus.
May every flower bloom it, Jesus.
May every bird sing it, Jesus.
May every person proclaim it, Jesus.
May every life reflect it, Jesus.

Jesus, His Name will sound through the corridors of time and in eternity like the music of all choirs poured forth in one anthem.

When the pearls have lost their luster,
When the sun has lost its brilliance,
When the moon has lost its clearness,
When the birds have lost their melody,
When the honeybee has lost its sweetness,
The Name of Jesus will still be resounding.

His Name brings peace, joy, and happiness.
His Name gives purpose, direction, contentment, and fulfillment.

Chapter 20

The Love of God

Love is strong affection. Love is passionate affection. The characteristics of love are promptitude, thoroughness, self-denial, and unwavering patience. The manifestations of love include a compassionate heart, an attentive look, willing feet, and helpful hands.

Take a look at the Love of God:

An everlasting love: Jeremiah 31:3 *"Yea, I have loved thee with an everlasting love."*

An incomparable love: John 15:13 *"Greater love hath no man than this, that a man lay down his life for his friends."*

An unsurpassed love: Romans 5:8 *"But God commendeth his love toward us, in that, while we were yet sinners, Christ died for us."*

An irrepressible love: Ephesians 2:4-5, NKJV, *"But God, who is rich in mercy, because of His great love with which He loved us, [5] even when we were dead in trespasses."*

An inseparable love: Romans 8:38-39 *"For I am persuaded, that neither death, nor life, nor angels, nor principalities, nor powers, nor things present, nor things to come, [39] Nor height, nor depth, nor any other creature, shall be able to separate us from the love of God, which is in Christ Jesus our Lord."*

An unlimited love: John 3:16 *"For God so loved the world, that he gave his only begotten Son, that whosoever believeth in him should not perish, but have everlasting life."*

Love for the denying Simon Peter.
Love for the outcast woman.
Love for the extortionate Zacchaeus.
Love for the doubting Thomas.
Love for the dying thief.
Love for you and love for me.

It is now 1:30 a.m., Sunday morning. Time to retire. Writing about the Love of God is exciting!

Chapter 21

When Is It Time to Repent

What is repentance? To feel regret over action or intention: a changing of one's mind; and, taking positive action.

When sin is in your life, it is time to repent! No options! When we hold ought against our brother, it is time to repent! When we harbor ill feelings such as malice and hatred in our hearts, it is time to repent! When we take advantage of our brother, our neighbors, etc., it is time to repent!

When we are more critical than complimentary, it is time to repent! When worldly things (fleshly and carnal) excite us more than spiritual things, it is time to repent! When we miss church without missing church, it is time to repent! When we shut up our bowels of compassion against the needy, it is time to repent!

When we are more concerned about the fashions of this world than the favor of God, it is time to repent! When we begin to conform to this vile world, it is time to repent!

Romans 12:1-2 *"I beseech you therefore, brethren, by the mercies of God, that ye present your bodies a living sacrifice, holy, acceptable unto God, which is your reasonable service.*
2 And be not conformed to this world: but be ye transformed by the renewing of your mind, that ye may prove what is that good, and acceptable, and perfect, will of God."

There is also repentance for Christians, for 'good' people. David, a man after God's own heart, said in 2 Samuel 12:13 *"I have sinned against the LORD."* He did not blame anyone.

Read Psalm 51:1-3,7-12 *"Have mercy upon me, O God, according to thy lovingkindness: according unto the multitude of thy tender mercies blot out my transgressions.*

2 Wash me throughly from mine iniquity, and cleanse me from my sin. 3 For I acknowledge my transgressions: and my sin is ever before me. 7 Purge me with hyssop, and I shall be clean: wash me, and I shall be whiter than snow.

8 Make me to hear joy and gladness; that the bones which thou hast broken may rejoice. 9 Hide thy face from my sins, and blot out all mine iniquities.

10 Create in me a clean heart, O God; and renew a right spirit within me. 11 Cast me not away from thy presence; and take not thy holy spirit from me. 12 Restore unto me the joy of thy salvation."

The Bible speaks of Job as being upright and perfect, fearing God and hating evil. Then, in Job 42:6, we hear Job saying, *"Wherefore I abhor myself, and repent in dust and ashes."*

Now hear the conclusion of this thought as recorded in 2 Chronicles 7:14, *"If my people, which are called by my name, shall humble themselves, and pray, and seek my face, and turn from their wicked ways; then will I hear from heaven, and will forgive their sin, and will heal their land."*

Chapter 22

It Is Not the Place

Now the Lord can do His work anywhere. "It is not the place, it's what takes place."

Our Lord spoke a man out of a tree. He spoke a man out of a casket. He spoke a man out of a tomb. He spoke a man out of a bed of affliction.

He stretched forth His hand and healed a leprous man. He stretched forth His hand and healed a blind man. He stretched forth His hand and healed Simon Peter's mother-in-law. He touched her hand, and the fever left her. He spoke peace to a troubled sea, and there was a great calm.

The place makes no difference – a mountain, seashore, cemetery, house, roadside, or a ship.

I love Matthew 9:35, *"And Jesus went about all the cities and villages, teaching in their synagogues, and preaching the gospel of the kingdom, and healing every sickness and every disease among the people."*

The Lord is here! This is the time and place: to pour out your soul, to proclaim your hope, and to acknowledge your faith.

Let your heart be comforted.
Let your soul be cheered.
Let your spirit be exuberated.
Let your mind be refreshed.

Hear Psalm 77:13 *"Thy way, O God, is in the sanctuary."* God can do His business anywhere, even on the back side of the desert.

Psalm 122:1 *"I was glad when they said unto me, Let us go into the house of the LORD."*

Psalm 42:4 *"I went with them to the house of God, with the voice of joy and praise, with a multitude that kept holyday."*

Psalm 84:10 *"I had rather be a doorkeeper in the house of my God, than to dwell in the tents of wickedness."*

Chapter 23

When We Hear the Word Death

Death, we fear the most.
Death, we hate the most.
Death, we dread the most.

Death blights God's beautiful creation.
Death takes the bloom from the picture which the Divine Artist has penciled in.
Death withers the majestic tree which the Divine Gardener has planted.

Death, when we hear the word, the sun loses its brightness.
Death, when we hear the word, the moon loses its clearness.
Death, when we hear the word, the red roses lose their color.
Death, when we hear the word, the birds lose their melody.

We hang our harps on the willows by the streams of bereavement.
> We lose our joy.
> We lose our laughter.
> We lose our melody.

Some of these thoughts were used when I ministered at Carroll Ellison's funeral service. Brother Ellison was one of the leading musicians in the Church of God, in South Carolina.

What I have written in this message can be seen differently when _death_ is recognized as God's officer:

Death can awaken the careless.
Death can alarm the impenitent.
Death can arouse the backslider.
Death can excite the hope of a believer.
Death can be a release for the child of God. Hallelujah!

NO SET ORDER OF DEATH

We read in the Book of Genesis what seems to be the order of death in a family. Abraham gave up the ghost and died in a good old age; an old man; and, his sons buried him.

Isaac gave up the ghost, and died, being old and full of days; and, his sons buried him.

Jacob gathered up his feet into his bed, and yielded up the ghost; his sons carried him into the land of Canaan; and, buried him.

According to 2 Samuel 18, there was a change in this order for the Bible informs us that young Absalom, David's son, was slain. The King was much moved and went up to the chamber over the gate, and wept; and as he went, he said (Verse 33), *"O my son Absalom, my son, my son Absalom! would God I had died for thee, O Absalom, my son, my son!"*

We associate courage, strength, and alertness with the young. It would seem that such characteristics could evade death, but how many times have we been reminded that age makes no difference? Often the young are called first, and the order is changed, and we cry, *"My son, my son, would God I had died for thee, my son, my son."*

Part IV

Meditations

Chapter 24

Be Ye Stedfast

1 Corinthians 15:58 *"Therefore, my beloved brethren, **be ye stedfast**, unmoveable, always abounding in the work of the Lord, forasmuch as ye know that your labour is not in vain in the Lord."*

Hear Paul's testimony in 2 Timothy 4:6-7, *"For I am now ready to be offered, and the time of my departure is at hand. [7] I have fought a good fight, I have finished my course, I have kept the faith."*

Now hear Paul's admonition to us in 1 Timothy 6:12, *"Fight the good fight of faith, lay hold on eternal life, whereunto thou art also called, and hast professed a good profession before many witnesses."*

Don't give up - don't surrender - don't quit. There may be *Just One More . . .*

- One more mountain to climb
- One more mile to go
- One more valley to forge
- One more giant to defeat
- One more temptation to face
- One more trial to engage
- One more fight to fight
- One more race to run
- One more problem to encounter
- One more heartache to bear
- One more devil to rebuke
- One more storm to endure
- One more river to cross

Canaan Land is just in sight!
The words will be heard, "Welcome Home, My Child."

Chapter 25

Let's Think of Jesus Christ

Jesus Christ, the only Begotten Son of God.
Jesus Christ, the Expressed Image of God.
Jesus Christ, the Visual Expression of God.
Jesus Christ, the Brightness of God's Glory.
Jesus Christ, the only True and Complete Revelation of God,
"He that hath seen me hath seen the Father," John 14:9.

Jesus Christ, the Mind of God thinking out to man.
Jesus Christ, the Voice of God calling out to man.
Jesus Christ, the Heart of God throbbing out to man.
Jesus Christ, the Arm of God reaching out to man.

Jesus Christ,
>   The Word of God,
>   The Son of God,
>   The Heir of God.

Jesus Christ,
>   The Lamb of God,
>   The Chosen of God,
>   The Gift of God.

Jesus Christ,
>   The Wisdom of God,
>   The Power of God,
>   The Almighty God.

Jesus Christ,
>   The Rose of Sharon,
>   The Lily of the Valley,
>   The Bright and Morning Star.

Chapter 26

Christ Makes the Difference

Isaiah 53:4,5 *"Surely he hath borne our griefs, and carried our sorrows: yet we did esteem him stricken, smitten of God, and afflicted. ⁵ But he was wounded for our transgressions, he was bruised for our iniquities: the chastisement of our peace was upon him; and with his stripes we are healed."*

Yes, Jesus Christ was –
>   Despised and Rejected
>   Oppressed and Afflicted
>   Wounded and Bruised, and
>   Carried as a lamb to the slaughter.

Yes, HE makes the difference –
>   In spite of every devil-whispered doubt
>   In spite of every negative circumstance
>   In spite of every bad medical report
>   In spite of every throbbing pain
>   In spite of every adverse condition of life.

Jesus is the One who makes the difference. So let Him have His way until the day is done. Knowing this should:

>   Relieve our worry
>   Alleviate our grief
>   Lessen our anxiety
>   Dispel our sorrow
>   Dissolve our frustration
>   Excite our hope
>   Encourage holy living among us.

Would you allow the Lord Jesus Christ to make a difference in your life? He is ready. Are you?

Chapter 27

Walking With the Lord

Walk with the Lord today,
   and He will walk with you tomorrow.

Walk with the Lord during the day,
   and He will walk with you during the night.

Walk with the Lord when others are around,
   and He will walk with you when no one is around.

Walk with the Lord in good times,
   and He will walk with you during bad (hard) times.

Walk with the Lord during days of good health,
   and He will walk with you during sickness. He will even
      make your bed during your sickness, Psalm 41:3.

Walk with Him (the Lord) on earth,
   and He will walk with you in Heaven.

Walk with Him in life,
   and He will walk with you in death. *"Yea, though I walk
      through the valley of the shadow of death, I will fear no
      evil: for thou art with me."* Psalm 23:4.

Walk with Him in time,
   and He will walk with you in eternity.

Oh! He walks with me,
And He talks to me,
And He tells me I am His own.
Oh the joy we share!

To talk with Him, no breath is lost. Talk on.
To wait on Him, no time is lost. Wait on.
To walk with Him, no strength is lost. Walk on.

Chapter 28

Wait on the Lord

Just a few lines from a lengthy poem . . .

> When care is passing you down a bit,
> Rest if you must, but don't you quit.
>
> Don't give up when the pace seems slow,
> You might succeed with another blow.
>
> Stick to the fight when you're hardest hit,
> It's when things seem worse that you must not quit.

Psalm 37:3-7
> "_Trust_ in the LORD, and do good."
> And you shall be fed.
>
> "_Delight_ thyself also in the LORD:
> And he shall give thee the desires of thine heart."
>
> "_Commit_ thy way unto the LORD; trust also in him;"
> And He shall fulfill His promises.
>
> "He shall bring forth thy righteousness as the light,
> And thy judgment as the noonday."
>
> " Rest in the LORD,
> And wait patiently for him."

He gives His love to constrain us.
He gives His grace to sustain us.
He gives His word to strengthen us. And,
He gives His Spirit to inspire us.

"Wait, I say, Wait on the Lord." Psalm 27:14.

"They that wait upon the LORD shall renew their strength; they shall mount up with wings as eagles; they shall run, and not be weary; and they shall walk, and not faint." Isaiah 40:31.

Part V

Sermon Thoughts

Chapter 29

God's Plan

When God is working His plan,

As with Moses,
>The King could not detain him,
>The sea could not restrain him.

As with Daniel and the Hebrew boys,
>Fire could not consume them,
>Lions could not devour them,
>Satan could not overthrow them.

As with Paul,
>Chains could not bind him,
>Jails could not hold him,
>Water could not drown him,
>Snakes could not harm him,
>Satan could not destroy him.

As with Jesus Christ,
>Satan could not seduce Him,
>Religious leaders could not detour Him,
>Death could not destroy Him, and
>The Grave could not keep Him.

God has a plan for your life.
>There is a fight to fight!
>There is a race to run!
>There is a course to finish!
>There is faith to keep!
>There is a crown to win!
>There is a plan to fulfill!

Chapter 30

Facing Life

There will be rivers to cross, wildernesses to experience, mountains to climb, giants to face, enemies to fight, and walls to encounter. But, the Lord will cause:

The rivers to seem like two-foot ditches,
The wildernesses to seem like an oasis,
The mountains to crumble,
The walled cities to fall down flat,
The giants to seem like midgets,
The enemies to scatter.

Some of you have gone through the waters.
  They did not overthrow you.
Some of you have gone through the fires.
  They did not consume you.
Some of you have gone through the storms.
  They did not destroy you.
Some of you have gone through tribulations.
  They did not overwhelm you.

Continue to be brave.
Continue to be obedient.
Continue to be constant.
Continue to be faithful.

Life will continue to impose measureless fears.
Life will continue to bring frustrations.
Life will continue to cripple vital forces.

Life will continue to fray nerves.
Life will continue to sap energies.

But hear the Word . . . I Corinthians 16:13 – *"Watch ye, stand fast in the faith, quit you like men, be strong."*

Keep on singing. Keep on praising.
Keep on worshipping. Keep on keeping on . . .
Hallelujah!

Chapter 31

Now

1 John 3:1-2 *"Behold, what manner of love the Father hath bestowed upon us, that we should be called the sons of God: therefore the world knoweth us not, because it knew him not.*
² *Beloved, **now** are we the sons of God, and it doth not yet appear what we shall be: but we know that, when he shall appear, we shall be like him; for we shall see him as he is."*

- It is not who we were, it is who we are, NOW!

- It is not what we did, it is what we are doing, NOW!

- It is not where we were, it is where we are, NOW!

- It is not where we have been, it is where we are going, NOW!

- It is not what we had, it is what we have, NOW!

- It is not what we said, it is what we are saying, NOW!

- It is not how we acted, it is how we are acting, NOW!

- It is not how we appeared, it is how we appear, NOW!

- It is not what we gave, it is what we are giving, NOW!

- It is not how we talked, it is how we are talking, NOW!

- It is not how we walked, it is how we are walking, NOW!

Now is the time to make your calling and election sure - *"Brethren, give diligence to make your calling and election sure."* 2 Peter 1:10.

Now is the best time to consider - *"That if thou shalt confess with thy mouth the Lord Jesus, and shalt believe in thine heart that God hath raised him from the dead, thou shalt be saved."* Romans 10:9.

Chapter 32

Grace

Grace is undeserved favor.

All grace is from the Lord and in the Lord, essentially, abundantly, unchangeably, and eternally.

The Lord has grace for all. John 1:16, *"And of his fulness have all we received, and grace for grace."*

The Lord has grace for the church. Acts 4:33, *"And with great power gave the apostles witness of the resurrection of the Lord Jesus: and great grace was upon them all."*

The Lord has grace for the individual. 2 Corinthians 12:9 (Paul's testimony), *"My grace is sufficient for thee."*

Grace and Mercy seem to operate hand in hand with each other. Grace is getting what we do not deserve. Mercy is not getting what we rightfully deserve.

Read this beautiful Scripture found in 1 Timothy 1:1-2, *"Paul, an apostle of Jesus Christ by the commandment of God our Saviour, and Lord Jesus Christ, which is our hope; 2 Unto Timothy, my own son in the faith: Grace, mercy, and peace, from God our Father and Jesus Christ our Lord."*

Grace for you and grace for me.
Grace so full and grace so free.
Grace for today and grace for tomorrow.
Grace for time and grace for eternity.
Grace for life and grace for death.
Grace for earth and grace for heaven.

"That in the ages to come he might shew the exceeding riches of his grace in his kindness toward us through Christ Jesus." Ephesians 2:7.

Praise God for Grace, Mercy, Peace, and Hope!

Chapter 33

How Much Do You Desire

Ephesians 3:20 - *"Now unto him that is able to do exceeding abundantly above all that we ask or think, according to the power that worketh in us."*

- We ask for a cup full, and God wants to give us a barrel full.
- We ask for a spark, and God wants to give us cloven tongues of fire.
- We ask for a snack, and God wants to give us an all-you-can-eat platter.
- We ask for a sprinkle, and God wants to give us a gulley washer.

Some of us cannot get all of His blessings because we have not made room for them. Some of us cannot get all of His blessings because we keep the windows of heaven closed (tithe). Some of us cannot get all of His blessings because we have not obeyed Him (His Word).

God is able: Able to do how much? Exceedingly, abundantly, above, beyond a limit, more than enough. Let me refer you to the Ditch Digging Story found in 2 Kings, Chapter 3.

The setting was the Valley of Edom (the wilderness of Edom). Jehoshaphat and the children of Israel were not only faced by an enemy (the Moabites) but were also in dire need of water. The prophet of the Lord informed them to "make ditches." They made ditches, and the valley was filled with water.

Maybe you need to dig a spiritual ditch. Seek the Lord. Discover what He wants you to do.

Chapter 34

What a Day!

What a day it was when God came down on Sinai's melting summit amid lightning bolts, deafening thunders, heaving earthquakes, and He launched the Mosaic dispensation.

What a day it was when the covey of golden-winged angels flew around the Mount of Bethlehem and announced to the humble shepherds that the Christ of Glory was born.

What a day it was when Christ was nailed to the cross, the sun withdrew its light, the veil of the Temple was rent from top to bottom, the earth quaked, and screams filled the air as dead saints walked the streets.

What a day it was when that same Jesus arose from the dead, came out of the tomb, rattling the keys of death and hell, saying, *"I am he that liveth, and was dead; and, behold, I am alive for evermore, Amen."* Revelation 1:18.

What a day it was when the Third Person of the Trinity took up the reins of government – the sound came as a mighty rushing wind and filled the Upper Room where believers were waiting; cloven tongues came and sat upon each of them; they were filled with the Holy Ghost and began to speak that heavenly language as the Spirit gave them utterance.

What a day it is going to be when 1 Thessalonians 4:16-17 is fulfilled. *"For the Lord himself shall descend from heaven with a shout, with the voice of the archangel, and with the trump of God: and the dead in Christ shall rise first: Then we which are alive and remain shall be caught up together with them in the clouds, to meet the Lord in the air: and so shall we ever be with the Lord."*

Chapter 35

Just Thoughts – Let's Live

A life of meaning, not misery.
A life of certainty, not chance.
A life of fullness, not failure.
A life of assurance, not anxiety.
A life of faith, not fear.
A life of victory, not defeat.

May we accept our portion.

Just Thoughts – Success

Success is failure turned inside out,
The silver tint of the clouds of doubt,
And you never can tell how close you are.
It may be near when it seems afar.
So stick to the fight when you are hardest hit,
It's when things seem worse that you must not quit.

Defeat and disappointment don't equal failure. Happenings don't mean failure – they are not final. They can be helpful. They can reshape the course of your life. They can be the essentials to your success. They can be blessings in disguise.

They don't have to be ends; they can be means.

Just Thoughts – Make Melody

Ephesians 5:18-19 – *"Be filled with the Spirit; Speaking to yourselves in psalms and hymns and spiritual songs, singing and making melody in your heart to the Lord."*

We bear our pain.
We suffer our disappointments.
We carry our burdens.
We face death and we shed our tears.
But we have a song - - - We must sing it! - - -
    We must make melody!

"There's within my heart a melody,
Jesus whispers sweet and low.
Fear not I am with thee
In all of life's ebb and flow."

The shadows of night fall around us, the dark hours are sometimes long, and seasons of trouble often engulf us. But Job 35:10 declares that God gives songs in the night.

Keep on singing!

Just Thoughts - Going

We started here in tears,
    but we are going to arrive yonder in triumph.
We started here in weakness,
    but we are going to arrive yonder in power.
We started here in corruption,
    but we are going to arrive yonder in incorruption.

We started here in time,
    but we are going to arrive yonder in eternity.
We started here in the flesh,
    but we are going to arrive yonder in the Spirit.

Just Thoughts - Hope

The power of hope:

> Hope will enable us to live in our pain.
> Hope will enable us to live through our pain.
> Hope will enable us to live beyond our pain.

So, claim hope!
Embrace hope!
Give hope a chance!

Just Thoughts – Death

When the word "death" is heard,
    The sun may be shining brightly in the sky.
    The roses may be blooming ever so beautifully in the garden.
    The birds may be singing most melodiously in the trees.

Yet when the word "death" is heard,
    The sun loses its brightness,
    The blossoming red roses lose their color, and,
    The melody of the birds is not heard.

We hang our hopes on the willows by the streams of bereavement,
We lose our joy.
We cease our laughter.
And suddenly, we find ourselves behind banks of darkness and bereavement.

Just Thoughts – God's Presence

It was the Presence of the Lord that turned the backside of the desert into a sanctuary as the bush burned without being consumed to encourage and direct Moses.

It was the Presence of the Lord that turned the Egyptian jail into a university to prepare Joseph to occupy the position next to Pharaoh.

It was the Presence of the Lord that turned the cemetery of Gadara into a healing station.

It was the Presence of the Lord that turned the Isle of Patmos into a heavenly dreamland when John had been banished there to die.

It was the Presence of the Lord that turned the Philippian jail into a revival center after Paul and Silas had been beaten and placed in stocks. At midnight (Acts 16:25), they prayed and sang praises unto God, and the prisoners heard them.

Psalms 139:7 – *"Whither shall I go from thy spirit? or whither shall I flee from thy presence?"* What did the Psalmist say – *"Yea, though I walk through the valley of the shadow of death, I will fear no evil: for thou art with me."*

Praise the Lord for His Presence!

Just Thoughts – Divine Intervention

When did the Lord open the Red Sea?

When did the Lord open up a self-replenishing supermarket in the widow's house of Zarephath? (1 Kings 17).

When did the Lord break the captivity of famine in Samaria? (2 Kings 6-7).

When did the Lord turn the fiery furnace into an autumn breeze for the Hebrew boys?

When did the Lord heal the woman with the issue of blood?

When did the Lord save Paul and the other 275 during the stormy voyage to Rome?

The answer to the 'when' is - - - when all hope was seemingly gone.

Just Thoughts – First Base

Matthew 6:33 – *"Seek ye first the kingdom of God."*

A noted baseball player swung the bat. An infield hit went to the corner of the ballpark and rattled around. The outfielder had difficulty retrieving the ball.

The crowd arose. The shouting was loud. The batter ran the bases with the running coach waving him on.

Around first base, then around second base, then around third base, then to home plate. Oh! What a scene! An infield hit that resulted in a homerun.

The crowd almost went crazy with excitement!

In a matter of minutes, the pitcher finally received the ball. The pitcher then threw the ball to the first baseman. The first baseman tagged the first base. The first base umpire cried, "Out!"

The homerun, or what seemed to be a home run, was not a home run. The hitter (the runner) did not tag first base.

Whatever you do in life is worthless unless and until you tag first base: not by it, not over it, and not around it. It must be tagged first!

Part IV

Funeral Sermons

Chapter 36

The Funderburk Family
It is Almost Midnight – December 8, 2023

My mind goes back a few years to December 26, 2015. It was midnight for the Funderburk family. Their son, Robert "Rob" Funderburk, age 46, passed away.

Bishop Gerald Funderburk and Joyce, his wife, have been my acquaintances most of our lives. Gerald and I are from the same town and church, Fort Mill, South Carolina. Our dads were very close buddies in the same town, the same cotton mill, and the same church. Gerald and I have worked together in the Mauldin Church of God for about ten years. Now, both of us are enjoying retirement.

I have observed this couple many times, looked at them in church, worshipped with them, worked hand in hand with them, and sometimes have thought, "How are they going to make it? How are they going to survive their son's death?"

I am writing this message tonight for someone because you have lost a child in death. We must not deny it. Death hurts! The death of a child hurts worse, so I am told. We live in a real world, a hard world, a painful world, an injurious world, a devastating world.

We grieve! Life is interrupted by death. Cry! Cry big tears! Grief is love's price. Deep love causes deep grief. The only way to miss grief is to miss love. The only way to avoid grief is to avoid love. Grief is love's inevitable price. Grief is the aftermath of any deeply felt loss.

There is no way for us to know how much Brother and Sister Funderburk have grieved these past few years. How have they survived? They have claimed hope. Hope is a word; hope is a state; hope is a condition; hope is an experience. Look to Hebrews 11:1, *"Now faith is the substance of things hoped for, the evidence of things not seen."*

To me, hope not only gives assurance but **is** assurance. The feeling that what is desired will happen!

In Romans 5:5, we read that hope is not shameful.

In Romans 15:4, we read that we have hope through the comfort and patience of the Scripture.

In 2 Corinthians 1:7, we read of stedfast hope.

In Colossians 1:4-5, we read of reserved hope.

In Colossians 1:23, we read that we should continue to be grounded in faith and hope.

So, how have the Funderburks survived? They have claimed hope. They have embraced hope. They have given hope a chance.

Hope has enabled them to live in their pain.
Hope has enabled them to live through their pain.
Hope has enabled them to live beyond their pain.
Hope has enabled them to press onward.

This same hope has been real for others who have faced the grief of a child's death. I recall many in my pastorate years, such as:

Charlene Cannon, daughter of Junior & Doris Cannon
Gene McKenzie, son of Elton & Pauline McKenzie
George Case, son of C Casey & Mary Case
J. W. Frierson, son of Sara Frierson
Ronnie Starling, son of James & Edna Starling
Ronnie Howard, son of Fred & Marie Howard
Dan Ward, Jr., son of Dan & Bare Ward
Van Chandler, son of Pete & Christie Chandler
Tony Griffin, son of Melvin Griffin

I dedicate this message to all these families.

Chapter 37

Bishop Richard Case

A Memorial and Appreciation Day for the Reverend Richard Case, his wife, Becky, his family, and the Cleveland, South Carolina, Church of God.

The clock here at the Johnson house, December 10, 2023, is racing toward midnight. It is time to write!

More than fifty-five years ago, my wife, Peggy, and I accepted the Florence, South Carolina, Church as pastor. We became acquainted with some of the most wonderful people in the Church of God. We were met by the James Starling family, the Polks, the Tanners, the Stepps, the Cookes, the Lewis', the Barrentines, and the Cases. Most of these dear folk have departed this life, except James and Edna Starling, who are dear to my heart.

After giving you this family introduction, I refer you to the Case and Barrentine families and commence my message.

The title is: Essentials for a Church. The essentials for a church involve three things: Pastor, Place, and People.

PASTOR
Coming from the Case and Barrentine families were two fighting youngsters, Ricky and Becky. They fought as children; they fought as youths; and finally, they quit fighting and married each other.

Ricky could have remained in Florence with his young, beautiful wife. He had a good future there as part of his dad's business. But after a few years of life wrestling, he and Becky felt the call to ministry. Today's setting started about 38 – 40 years ago, as they agreed to move to these hills. Now let me tell you about Ricky - this church, these hills, and his family brought much happiness to him.

Listen, there are times when sudden and unexpected changes come and our whole life is concentrated into one single day. Joy and sorrow, tears and laughter, all lie close together in the ever-changing experience of human life. The source of greatest joy is often turned into a channel through which flows the most bitter anguish.

Life to Ricky Case was a God-given opportunity to live, to labor, to love, and to laugh. Life to him was more than the imposing of time, more than the sapping of energy, and much more than outrages and indignities placed upon mankind, especially pastors.

Pastor Richard Case brought what he was to these hills. Let me tell you I knew this young man. He was one of the most accommodating men of my acquaintance; one of the most cheerful; one of the most warm-hearted; and, one of the most unselfish.

After God gave him thirty years in these hills as the faithful pastor of the Cleveland Church of God, He called him home. Before his departure, he made a difference here.

PLACE

Then I thought about the second important essential, the Place. As I thought about this place, the hills of Cleveland, South Carolina, I also thought about Jacob and his story recorded in Genesis, Chapter 28.

Jacob was on an untried journey. The Bible says that he lighted (came) upon a *"certain place."* And oh, what an experience that Jacob had – the ladder reaching from earth to heaven, the angels ascending and descending, and, the Lord standing at the top of the ladder. That place was so welcoming and wonderful to Jacob that he cried out in Genesis 28:17, *"And said, How dreadful is this place! this is none other but the house of God, and this is the gate of heaven."*

Now I don't know if Brother Case (always Ricky to me) got that excited or not when he first arrived in Cleveland. But listen, there was a time in yesteryear that trees grew everywhere around here along with the singing birds, the leaping deer, the howling wolves, and the jumping rabbits.

Then God brought people to these hills. Some of you are descendants of those folk. Then God brought preachers, evangelists, and then pastors. Church buildings were erected. Then around 38-40 years ago, the Reverend Richard and Becky came as your leaders.

PEOPLE

Now church, let me thank you for receiving them, for blessing them, for supporting them, all of these years.

Let me thank you Sister Mary Case, dear Mother, for releasing him.

Let me thank you Rebecca Barrentine Case for remaining by his side.

Let me thank you children, in-laws, and grands for hanging close to him.

The Lord has called him home. Our hearts are heavy. He loved us and we loved (love) him.

Our grief is heavy, but we have hope. Remember my former remarks on the subject of grief. But more, remember my former remarks on hope. I urge you to claim hope today.

Note: I have included Brother Ricky's funeral message in this book because his family is one of the dearest families of my pastorate. I served as his family's pastor for twelve years and extended service for more than 40 years.

I served as the pastor of his grandparents, his parents, and three brothers. I preached funeral sermons for his grandparents, his parents, two brothers, and extended family members, as well as conducted several marriages.

Well, midnight has almost caught me again.
Goodnight!
The Ole Bishop.

Chapter 38

Louise Sanders

The Funeral Sermon for the Louise Sanders Service (Sweet and Low), February 26, 2020.

We appreciate your being here this afternoon as we celebrate the beautiful journey of Sister Louise Sanders.

Her journey on this earth began over 93 years ago. It is as the Psalmist declared in Psalm 90:9-10, *"For all our days are passed away . . . we spend our years as a tale that is told. The days of our years are threescore years and ten; and if by reason of strength they be fourscore years, yet is their strength labour and sorrow; for it is soon cut off, and we fly away."*

Sister Louise, passing the *fourscore* (80) by 13 years felt as the Psalmist did sometimes in Psalm 55:6, *"Oh that I had wings like a dove! for then would I fly away, and be at rest."*

But listen, she continued her journey. Sometimes her journey was interrupted by physical maladies which were agonizing to the body, but she continued her journey.

Sometimes her journey was interrupted by seasons of providential darkness which were disturbing to the soul, but she continued.

Sometimes her journey was interrupted by trials and temptations which were perplexing to the spirit, but she continued.

The reason she continued through all of the circumstances of life is found in 1 Corinthians 15:58, *"Therefore, my beloved, be ye stedfast, unmoveable, always abounding in the work of the Lord."*

Her maximum height was 4'1", but she was stedfast, unmoveable, and always abounding the work of the Lord.

Her faithfulness to the Lord, her family, and her church is newsworthy. She was one of the nine faithful members of the Mauldin Church of God when I became their pastor 18 years ago.

Her life was enriched by the Holy Spirit of God. She was Pentecostal. She was spirit-filled. Being spirit-filled makes a difference in a person's earthly journey.

Her morals were high. Her convictions were strong. Her complaints were few. She lived the Christian life. She lived a victorious life! She has completed her journey in victory. Hear what she has just experienced at the end of this earthly journey. 1 Corinthians 15:54-57,

"Death is swallowed up in victory.
O death, where is thy sting? O grave, where is thy victory?
The sting of death is sin; and the strength of sin is the law.
But thanks be to God, which giveth us (me)
the victory through our Lord Jesus Christ."

Now, she would say 1 Corinthians 15:58 to all, friends and family, *"Therefore, my beloved, be ye stedfast, unmoveable, always abounding in the work of the Lord, forasmuch as ye know that your labour is not in vain in the Lord."*

Friends and Family, let the Lord that she served be:

- Your source of encouragement
- Your mighty weapon
- Your fountain of inspiration
- Your haven of rest and comfort

Let me add: the distresses, the depression, and the disturbances of life and death cannot prevail over those who have anchored their souls in the Haven of Rest.

Your journey can be victorious as hers was! Remember:

The Lord is stronger than circumstances,
The Lord is mightier than sin,
The Lord is wiser than satan.

Note: I included Sister Sander's funeral sermon in this book because she was one of the four supporters that was striving to keep the doors open at the Mauldin Church of God when I became the pastor.

Chapter 39

Elmer Totherow's Funeral Service Message

Elmer lived a full life. My first remembrance of Elmer is about 68 years ago. He was around 19 years of age, and I was about 12. We were working on the farms on Doby Bridge Road. This was the time when farmers helped each other, pay or no pay.

Much of my summertime was spent with my Grand-Dad Patterson, just about 100 yards from my birthplace, the ole Collins farmhouse. The Phillips/Bennett farmhouse was located just across the ole dirt road.

None of us in those farm days of yesteryear had much, but most of us had a place to sleep and food to eat. I recall some of that time Elmer had no place to sleep. Sometimes the ground was his couch, and the stars were his companions. Those adverse and trying circumstances did not keep him down or hold him back. During those times, God gave him a talent. That talent was called 'work.' I think it was Thomas Edison who said, "Success comes by 2% inspiration and 98% perspiration." (Sweat).

In the early years of his life, Elmer accepted Jesus Christ as his Lord and Savior. Two saintly ladies of the Fort Mill Church of God, Sister Perry and Sister Langley, played a vital role in his living a Christian life.

Live a Christian life,
Men will admire you,
Women will respect you, and,
God will crown your life with success.
And when the twilight of your life mingles
With the purpling dawn of eternity,
Men will speak your name with honor
And baptize your grave with tears,
As God attunes for you the evening chimes.

I also feel that during those days of deprivation, God added another talent to his life – making money. It was amazing during his manhood he could set up a business, any kind and anywhere, and it would be successful. People seemingly enjoyed spending money at his places of business.

Elmer, who was married to my sister, Sara, provided well, extremely well, for his family. He supported the Lord's work, he supported my ministry, he blessed preachers, he paid people's electric bills, he put food on people's tables, and, he provided transportation (vehicles) for many.

One of the very noticeable characteristics of Elmer was his laughter. He knew what the wise preacher said in Proverbs 17:22, *"A merry heart doeth good like a medicine."* Elmer had a merry heart. His merry heart has been medicine for many. His smile and laughter often turned wrath and also served to heal in many situations. People enjoyed being around him and with him. He was a people person.

Now, I want us to consider two things: What death has done, and what the Lord has done.

Death has disrupted our homes.
Death has wrought havoc among us.
Death has crumbled our dreams.
Death has interrupted our lives.

But, the Lord has released Elmer from this earthly life. The Lord has transferred Elmer from earth to heaven. The Lord has presented Elmer to Himself. The Lord has received Elmer to Himself.

Jude, Verse 25 – *"Now unto him* (the Lord) *that is able to keep you from falling, and to present you faultless before the presence of his glory with exceeding joy."*

Now, what is the Lord doing for us, the family of Elmer? HE is giving us courage and grace to live our lives as Elmer lived out his life.

Let us Embrace Hope.
Let us Claim Hope.
Let us Allow Hope to work in our lives.

Closing Prayer

Funeral Service – December 3, 2015, Fort Mill Church of God

Note: I have conducted many funerals in my family, but Elmer was like a brother to me. He supported my ministry all the way.

Chapter 40

Boyce Clardy

July 26, 2016 - Simpsonville Church of God

Funeral Service Message of Boyce Clardy

We have assembled this morning because death has intruded again into our lives. Dark and heavy are the clouds that hang over us today as sadness and sorrow fill our hearts. Although the sun is shining brightly in the sky, the sun of our life seems to be set behind banks of darkness, and it is difficult to see rays of light.

Yet, the Lord Jesus Christ became clouded in our darkness to give us light, and, He was wounded in our sorrow to give us comfort. Therefore, may we repose our entire confidence in Him today and find grace to help amidst this darkness and bereavement.

May Proverbs 27:1 be noted as we commence our presentation, *"Thou knowest not what a day may bring forth."*

It is astonishing how many years of joy and sorrow can be concentrated into a single day.

A day can begin with a beautiful sunrise and end with a gloomy sunset.

A day can begin with laughter and end with weeping.

A day can begin in life and end in death.

Such as the passing of our friend and brother, Boyce Clardy. He was:

- A loving companion
- A considerate brother
- A patient granddad
- A steady worker
- A successful businessman
- A faithful church person.

Boyce lived and labored for others - his family, his friends, and strangers. People loved him. People trusted him. People relied upon him. People wanted to be around him.

The reason for all of this is found in Proverbs 15:1-2, *"A soft answer turneth away wrath: The tongue of the wise useth knowledge aright."* Boyce knew how to converse with people. He knew how to deal with people.

<u>Lastly, let me share this with you</u>. Boyce, his wife, Edna, and I started the Word of Life, Westwood Church in Simpsonville. We not only planted (started the church), but we helped to erect the first building. Edna became the Church Clerk. That church is now one of our most thriving churches today with 18 nationalities.

Boyce Clardy was one of my dearest friends.
He lived – He labored – He laughed.
His pride and joy sit before me today.
Edna, Wanda, and Allen – God bless you.
You were his life.

Note: I included this Funeral Service in this book because the Clardy family was dear to me. Boyce and his wife, Edna, helped me to start and build the Word of Life Church in Simpsonville, South Carolina, which has become one of our strong churches. Boyce's brother, Ken, was my church clerk at Liberty, South Carolina. Ken was also my friend and buddy.

Chapter 41

John Littlejohn

I just told Phyllis I am going to my study for a few minutes and then to bed. As I sat down at my desk, I thought about Brother Littlejohn. It is almost midnight, but I must write a few minutes.

Brother Littlejohn was a fighter. From childhood to this death, he was a fighter. When we hear about his childhood, we conclude he was a fighter.

When we hear about his young adulthood, he was a fighter, a military man. He fought for you and me.

When we hear about his physical condition, cirrhosis of the liver at age 30, he fought through life. (He was not an alcoholic man, his disease was not caused by such).

When we hear about his successful business as a Building Contractor, we conclude he was a fighter.

As we witnessed his journey these past three years - the suffering, the physical agony, the painful treatments that he encountered – we are ready to declare, John Littlejohn was a fighter.

I am convinced that there were times during his childhood when he felt like the psalmist of Psalm 55:6, *"Oh that I had wings like a dove! for then would I fly away, and be at rest."* He could not fly away during those fighting times, but now he can say, in Verse 18, *"God hath delivered my soul in peace from the battle that was against me."*

And, he can say as Paul, the Apostle, *"Thanks be to God, which giveth us the victory through our Lord Jesus Christ."* 1 Corinthians 15:57.

Sister Littlejohn (Sylvia), and family, you have been faithful to him. He lived for God and you.

Note: I was asked to preach at Brother Littlejohn's funeral, but I was ill and could not be there. The above message remarks were recorded for the service.

Chapter 42

D. H. Derrick

Why are we here this afternoon? Why have so many people gathered here this afternoon? Why is there such a beautiful crowd of people standing around this place today? This is a cemetery. Why are so many people here today at Hillcrest Cemetery, Greer, South Carolina?

We are here, first of all, because of life. Yes, we have assembled here today in this cemetery because of life.

The Life of D. H. Derrick.
Genesis 1:11 gives the origin of plant life.
Genesis 1:20 gives the origin of animal life.
Genesis 2:7 gives the origin of human life.
So, we are here today because the Lord gave human life, the life of D. H. Derrick.

Secondly, we are here today because of death, the death of D. H. Derrick. We are here today because this is the thing that family and friends do when there is a death.
This is what civilized people do.
This is what families do.
This is what friends do.
This is what comrades in the faith do.

Now, let me tell you about D. H. Derrick. He was a Bible-believing, Bible-practicing, praying man. In fact, he was one of the first men to join the Sunday Morning Prayer Group with the central thought to pray for the Pastor and Church when Brother Miles Mauldin pulled the group together. Derrick continued with that group until God called him home.

Derrick, as most people called him, was one of the most faithful church members of all my pastorates. He was one of the hardest working men of my acquaintance, honest in his work, and with a genuine concern for his fellow man.

One of his greatest attributes, if not his greatest, was his love and care for his wife, Joyce. I have never seen a man who fulfilled the words found in the Book of Ephesians, Chapter 5, more than Derrick. Hear the words in Verse 25, *"Husbands, love your wives, even as Christ also loved the church, and gave himself for it."*

Joyce loved him in return. Together as husband and wife, they enjoyed life with each other. Their happy times in life included blessing others. They had no children, but they blessed more people during my 35 years of acquaintance with them than any couple of all my pastorates.

We are here to celebrate his life!

Note: Haston Derrick was one of my dearest friends. I doubt if anyone loved me more than Haston.

Chapter 43

Why Ronny?
In Memory

Ronald Blake Starling, son of James and Edna Starling, was born August 17, 1957, in Rocky Mount, North Carolina. The family moved to Florence, South Carolina, in 1958. Ronny was seven years of age when I became his pastor in 1964 at the Florence Church of God.

For twelve years I saw Ronny's growing into young manhood as one of the most gentle, obedient, industrial, intellectual acquaintances of my life. At the age of 22, on September 26, 1979, Ronny was involved in a log truck accident and was taken into eternity. There is no way to understand it.

Why Ronny? He was a dedicated Christian, obedient to the Word of God.

Why Ronny? He was highly educated. He earned an Arc Welding Certificate from the Florence-Darlington Technical College in 1977 for 88 hours of credit. He earned a Bachelor of Science degree from Francis Marion College in 1979.

Why Ronny? He was a diligent and faithful church worker. The Florence Church purchased two buses and developed bus routes. Ronny was given one of the buses and one of the routes. He serviced his bus. He painted his bus

(Big Red). He kept up his bus, at times spending his own money, and worked his route.

Why Ronny? He was a musician, a church band member, and a singer.

Why Ronny? He was one of the most trustworthy young men of my acquaintance. I owned a house located at the Florence Oakdale Golf Course. I gave him a key to my house and the responsibility for the house when I moved from the church in Florence to the State Office, Mauldin, South Carolina.

Why Ronny? I cried today over his departure as I recorded the words that you just read.

Part VII

Excerpts from Funeral Sermons

Chapter 44

Excerpt from Funeral Sermon

My Friend, Tony Griffin

Allow me to read an unusual verse of Scripture for this excerpt. 1 Peter 2:9 - *"But ye are a chosen generation, a royal priesthood, an holy nation, a peculiar people; that ye should __shew forth__ the praises of him who hath called you out of darkness into his marvelous light."*

My friend, Tony Griffin, showed forth!

- He showed the world that there is hope in distress.
- He showed the world that there is help in despair.
- He showed the world that there is calmness in a disturbance.
- He showed the world that there is faith in the time of fear.
- He showed the world that there is victory in the time of warfare.
- He showed the world that there is relief in the time of heartache.
- He showed the world that there is strength in the time of weakness.

Tony was a gift from the Lord.
Tony was a single man, a gift, a special gift from the Lord.
Some people are very selfish with the Gift of Life . . . not Tony!

Tony was very generous with his Gift of Life. Tony gave out his gift, the Gift of Life. He gave his life out in love.

Chapter 45

Excerpt from Funeral Sermon

Billy Ray Gilbert

Acquaintances roll through my mind tonight as I sit at my desk and listen to the cracking of thunder.

I became acquainted with Billy Ray Gilbert more than forty years ago at the Park Place Church of God, Greenville, South Carolina, where I preached a revival. He was one of my converts. I also had the opportunity to baptize him in water during that week.

Brother Billy Ray, Authalene, his wife, and their boys transferred to Praise Cathedral when we started that new church. He and I spent many, many hours working together on the new buildings. He was not only talented in his work, but he was also a hard and faithful worker.

Look at some Scriptures that fit Billy Ray:
- Psalm 42:4 *"I went with them to the house of God, with the voice of joy and praise."*
- Psalm 77:13 *"Thy way, O God, is in the sanctuary."*
- Psalm 122:1 *"I was glad when they said unto me, Let us go into the house of the Lord."*

I knew him well. He never raised his voice. He never gossiped. He never spoke foolishly. He had a soft voice, a meek walk, and a tender spirit.

Thank the Lord for such a man.

Note: I included this message because of love.

Chapter 46

Excerpt from Funeral Sermon

Joe Hood - The Bible Says

How many times did Bishop Joe Hood say, "The Bible Says"?

Brother Hood read the Bible; he studied it; he shared it; he declared it; he preached it; and, if you pushed a little, he would argue it. He also taught it and debated it.

As I thought of his love for the Word of God, I turned to the Book of 2 Timothy and lifted some Scriptures.

2 Timothy 2:15 *"Study to shew thyself approved unto God, a workman that needeth not to be ashamed, rightly dividing the word of truth."*

2 Timothy 2:23-24 *"But foolish and unlearned questions avoid, knowing that they do gender strifes. 24 And the servant of the Lord must not strive; but be gentle unto all men, apt to teach, patient."*

2 Timothy 3:14-17 *"But continue thou in the things which thou hast learned and hast been assured of, knowing of whom thou hast learned them; 15 And that from a child thou hast known the holy scriptures, which are able to make thee wise unto salvation through faith which is in Christ Jesus. 16 All scripture is given by inspiration of God, and is profitable for doctrine, for reproof, for correction, for instruction in righteousness: 17 That the man of God may be perfect, thoroughly furnished unto all good works."*

Brother Hood would talk or preach the Word at the drop of a hat, and he would drop the hat. 2 Timothy 4:2 *"Preach the word; be instant in season, out of season; reprove, rebuke, exhort with all longsuffering and doctrine."*

Bishop Joe Hood was obedient to the Word.

Note: I included this message excerpt to excite you to read and study The Word, as Joe did along with Nellie, his wife, whom we all loved dearly and who studied for hours and hours with Joe.

Chapter 47

Excerpt from Funeral Sermon

Gene Gore

I am pleased to inform you that by the mercy of God, Gene was given time in life to get ready for death.

Time is Limited Duration

    The clock of life is wound but once
    And no man has the power
    To tell just when the hand will stop
    At late or early hour.
    Now is the only time we have
    So let us labor, live, and love with will
    And place no faith in tomorrow
    For the hand may then be still.

Right here in this sanctuary, Gene was given time and opportunity to prepare for eternity. Eternity is duration without limitation.

Now, allow me to remind you that you are at the right place and the right time to make the same preparation. Please take time before time takes you.

    Time is the pathway to eternity.
    Take time for eternity!
    Voice your concern.
    Confess your sin.
    Believe the Lord Jesus Christ!

Note: I included this message excerpt to show you the mercy of God.

Chapter 48

Excerpts from Funeral Messages

This chapter may seem somewhat strange. I wanted to include in this book some excerpts from funeral sermons, listing each of the deceased with excerpts, but how can one select twelve to fifteen of these from several hundred? So, I decided just to include funeral sermon excerpts without names.

Excerpt 1 - Continued

Please give attention to these words "She Continued."

- In spite of physical maladies which were agonizing to the body, she continued.
- In spite of seasons of provident darkness, she continued.
- In spite of trials and tempests which were perplexing to the mind, she continued.

She completed her journey on this earth in victory. Thanks be to God!

Excerpt 2 – She Knew Christ

She knew Christ.
She lived for Christ.
She lived the Christian life.

The tenderness in her spirit,
The softness in her voice,
The meekness in her walk,
The kindness in her actions,
The love in her expressions –
All gave indisputable evidence that she was a Christian – that she was Christ-like.

Excerpt 3 – What She Was

She was a lady of love in a world of hate.
She was a lady of warmth in a world of coldness.
She was a lady of cheerfulness in a world of gloom.
She was a lady of generosity in a world of greed.
She was a lady of character in a world of sinfulness.

Excerpt 4 – She Was Careful

She was careful in her marriage. Her husband, after more than 60 years of marriage, would tell you that she was careful as a loving sweetheart, faithful wife, and a congenial helpmate.

She was careful as a mother. Ask any of her children. She did the proper things at the proper time for her children.

She was careful as a Christian, choosing the things of the Lord, serving as a musician in the church, and laboring beside her husband in senior work

Excerpt 5 – As A Christian

As a Christian, she . . .
> Adored God's greatness
> Enjoyed God's purity
> Revered God's justice
> Trusted in God's truth
> Rejoiced in God's grace, and
> Delighted in God's mercy.

As a Christian, she was faithful as a companion, a mother, a church lady, and a friend. Her daily prayer was: *"Lord, let me be a true expression of your love, mercy, and grace. May there be light shining from my spirit that brings warmth and hope to others, and glory to your Holy Name."*

Excerpt 6 – A True Mother

I sat with a mother and her three grown children one day as she shared the difficulties that confronted her during some of her years as a single mother. Then, before the conversation ended, she said, *"They have been worth it."* What a statement!

She was a true mother in the full sense of the word. She had a compassionate heart, an attentive look, willing feet, helpful hands, and unwavering patience.

She was devout, earnest, and sincere as a true mother.

She was devoted, dedicated, and loyal as a true mother.

Excerpt 7 – A Pastor's Wife

She was married to one of my dearest preacher friends.

She accepted the role of a pastor's wife. His place of ministry was her place of ministry, whether a town, a city, a village, or a rural community, desirable or undesirable.

The church parsonage was their residence regardless of size, condition, furnishings, and green or yellow walls.

His financial compensation was her compensation, sufficient or insufficient.

His preaching was her preaching, acceptable or unacceptable.

A pastor's wife must be dedicated, strong, and devoted to the cause of God. She was!

Excerpt 8 – All the Way

She was careful about things as Luke writes about Martha in the 10th Chapter of his book. As a pastor's wife, she left every parsonage in better shape than when they moved into it.

Not only was she careful about things, but she also chose that good part as Mary did (Luke Chapter 10) that was not taken away.

She lived her profession of faith "all the way." She maintained her Christian relationship and attitude "all the way." She held high her church teachings and beliefs "all the way."

The following poem fits her well.

> With patience in His love, I'll rest,
> And whisper that He knoweth best,
> And I am satisfied.
> Then clinging to the guiding Hand,
> A weakling in His strength I'll stand,
> Though I be sorely tried.
> Burdened with a load of care,
> He has promised me strength to bear,
> The trials that appear.
> So hiding pain away from sight,
> I'll let my life be fair and bright,
> While waiting for His call.

Excerpt 9 – She Made Room

Our dear sister made room for others.
> She made room for her husband.
> She made room for her children.
> She made room for her friends.
> She made room for her church.
> She made room for her pastor.
> But more so, she made room for the Lord.

The reason she made room for all of us is because she made room for the Lord.

She made room for the Lord and was filled with His unspeakable joy. She made room for the Lord and was filled with His peace, which passeth all understanding. She made room for the Lord and was filled with His love, which is everlasting.

Now, the Lord has made room for her. Hear John 14:1-2:

"Let not your heart be troubled: ye believe in God, believe also in me. In my Father's house are many mansions: if it were not so, I would have told you. I go to prepare a place for you."

Excerpt 10 – He Lived and Died in the Faith

He showed us that life is more than a struggle.
He showed us that life is more than a vexation of spirit.
He showed us that life is more than a predicament that precedes death.

He did not consider youth as a blunder.
He did not consider maturity a predicament.
He did not consider retirement as a regret.
He did not consider death as a finality.
He lived and died in the Faith!

He was Christ-like.
He gave visibility to the Lord's invisibility.
He gave credibility to the Lord's existence.
He mirrored the Lord.

His cause was sacred.
His course was steady.
His call was holy.
His concern was Christ-centered.
His compassion was overflowing.
His convictions were strong.
His complaints were few.

Excerpt 11 – Life and Death

Life continues to be the great mystery of the universe. Philosophers have pondered its meaning for many decades. Scientists have investigated its nature for centuries. Skeptics have disputed its origin for ages. But God said, *"Let there be life,"* and it was.

Death – The Bible declares that it is appointed unto man to die. Death is what we fear the most. Death is what we dread the most. Death is what we hate the most.

Ecclesiastes 8:8 – *"There is no man that hath power over the spirit to retain the spirit; neither hath he power in the day of death."*

The cohorts of death are ever on man's trail. Accidents, sicknesses, and diseases continue to blast human life with physical doom, instituting reigns of terror; crushing human hopes; and, overcoming survivors with anguish.

Excerpt 12 – Grief and Hope

Yes, we cry.

We live in a real world, a hard world. Many times our loss is heavy, even unbearable. We grieve. Yes, we grieve. We cry. Yes, we cry.

Grief is love's inevitable price. Deep love causes deep grief. The only way to miss grief is to miss love. The only way to avoid grief is to avoid love.

We suffer grief today because of love. But, we have hope. Hope enables us to live in our grief. And, that hope will enable us to live through our grief.

Go ahead, cry! Cry big tears, but let hope be your anchor. Our hope is made certain by the Resurrection of Jesus Christ, our Lord from death and the grave.

Let us hold tenaciously to our hope! Praise the Lord!

Part VIII

Special Features

Chapter 49

Phyllis' Story

All of us have a story. Yours won't be like mine, and mine will not be like someone else's. Pain, sorrow, and disappointment come to everyone. It is a part of this life here on earth. Even though my story has great sorrow, which I am about to share with you, I want to tell you that God has poured love, mercy, and untold blessings into my life. I could not tell this story without giving thanks to Him for all He has given to me.

Part One of My Story

When I was 24 years old, my father passed away unexpectedly at the age of 58. Early one morning, he was leaving to go to work. He was about to get in his car when he had a massive heart attack. My parents had planned to travel to South Carolina for a visit in a few months for a very special reason. I was pregnant with their first grandchild! Naturally, we were very excited. Sadly, my dad never got to meet any of his grandchildren. I was and always will be a daddy's girl. I was devastated by his death, and I wanted to crawl into a hole and not come back out. However, there was a baby on the way, and it was my job to take care of myself and that precious child. As it turns out, that baby was our beautiful Charlene.

I believe that motherhood does not begin the moment a child is born. I believe it begins while the mother is carrying the baby. God knew how broken I would be, and there was no coincidence in the timing. God gave me something to look forward to.

Part Two of My Story

Two years later, my mother found out she had cancer. She had a tumor on the side of her knee, and it grew to be quite large. One day she bumped it and caused it to hemorrhage. She was immediately taken to the hospital, and within a few days, she was facing very serious surgery - an above-the-knee amputation. This was the only way to save her life.

My sister, aunt, and I sat with her in Oakland, California's Oak Knoll Naval Hospital. As she awaited her surgery, she got out of bed and walked about. My aunt made a comment out of her hearing that I'll never forget. "That's the last time she'll ever walk on two feet again."

And it was . . . on this earth. God gave her almost 28 more years here with us, and we cherished those years. The best thing to happen through this tragedy was that she came back to the Lord shortly after the amputation. She was raised in South Carolina in the Church of God, but she had strayed from her faith. She got saved, and she meant business. She became a strong Christian and an inspiration to me. I have no doubt she's in Heaven today.

Part Three of My Story

This will be the most challenging part of my story for me to share. My late husband, Bud, was a minister in the

Pentecostal Holiness denomination. When he was 41 years old and I was 35 years old, we learned that he had cancer.

For weeks he had severe head pain. His doctor sent him to have a CAT scan and later an MRI. These tests confirmed that he had a brain tumor on both sides of the brain's frontal lobe. Surgery was planned, but the doctor did not have good news afterward. The surgeon told us that anything he might have done during the surgery would have caused Bud to die. After some days in the hospital, he came home. A few weeks later, he was back in the hospital due to extreme weakness. He was to be there for a few days, but those days turned into weeks.

Jesse was not even two years old when his daddy became sick. Chandra was four, and Charlene was 10. After staying night and day at the hospital for several days, I knew I could not continue with three young children. They needed a portion of my time. Things fell into somewhat of a schedule. My two sisters-in-law were so good at taking care of the children, and they and their families, along with Bud's parents, took turns at the hospital when I could not be there.

Monday through Friday, I always got to the hospital very early, waiting on the doctors as they made their rounds, hoping to have some good news and know everything going on with his care. I believe that the doctors did everything possible to save his life, but it was not meant to be. He took chemotherapy and radiation treatments. He had a stem cell transplant, which was a serious procedure in itself.
After 15 weeks in the hospital, the doctors decided to release him, but that was not to be either. Each night during those long weeks, I would go to bed wondering, "Will tonight be the night that I get that dreaded phone call?" The last day before

he was to be released from the hospital, I was in the room with him when he said to me as he looked towards the window, "Do you see that angel?"

I didn't see it, but I know that he truly did see an angel there. Perhaps it was the angel that would carry him home. That is what I believe.

I went home and made sure that everything was prepared for his arrival. The hospital bed was set up, and everything seemed to be ready. As I went to sleep that night, I remember thinking, "Finally, he is coming home, and it is time. It's time for him to come home." But that did not happen. At approximately two o'clock in the morning, I received that call. I was told Bud had experienced a brain hemorrhage and I needed to come to the hospital immediately. My brother-in-law, Charlene, my mother and I hurried to the hospital. Family came to stay with Chandra and Jesse.

At that time, there was a long hall to walk down on the fifth floor of the Greenville Memorial Hospital to get to the patients' rooms. The pastor who was filling in for Bud at our church lived closer to the hospital and arrived before us. He was at the other end of the long hall and began to walk toward us. His face said it all, "Bud is gone."

That moment in time will be forever etched in my memory. The doctor came and spoke with us, and I have to say I have the utmost respect for the surgeon, every oncologist, every nurse, and every person who had anything to do with his care. They put everything they had into saving his life.

Two months after his passing, the staff on the fifth floor of the GMH put together a Christmas party for our children. I have no words for kindness like that.

After the funeral, our lives fell into a routine, but there was such a void. I felt lost and alone, like someone on a deserted island. What do I do now? But I was not alone, and God had not deserted me. It can feel like it when your husband and the father of your children are no longer in the home and will never be there again.

Only once did God speak to me in words that were so real they were audible, saying, "You will be taken care of." I heard those exact words as plain as if someone stood directly in front of me and spoke them. We lacked for nothing and had no concerns financially, but the thought of raising three children all alone was daunting.

Bud's family lived around us, and they were wonderful! However, there was only so much they could do. My heart and soul longed to be in church. The children and I continued to attend where Bud had pastored, but it was very difficult to return there.

After some time, I decided we would visit somewhere on a Sunday night. But where? So many pastors and churches had rallied around our family during this time, including Ron Carpenter, Sr., who was the superintendent of our church, the Pentecostal Holiness denomination.

I decided to visit Praise Cathedral Church of God. One reason was that I had friends, a wonderful couple, who attended there and they had asked me to come to visit. The other reason was that Bobby Johnson and the staff had visited Bud just like he was one of their own church members. One of the staff would come by his room almost every day throughout Bud's entire stay in the hospital. This made a deep impression on me, so that's where we went to visit.

I soaked up every moment of that first service. The following Sunday night, we went back. Even though we were still attending our church for the other services, we attended the Sunday night service at Praise Cathedral for several weeks. I went forward at the end of one of these services for prayer, and Bobby Johnson prayed for me. We continued to attend, and eventually, Praise Cathedral became our home church.

I'll never forget the pastor, Gerald Johnson, who helped us so much during Bud's sickness and death and served as pastor until a permanent pastor was found. We still see him on occasion. He took part in our wedding along with two other ministers.

Who would have thought that someone would come into my life (Bobby Johnson) and not only take a wife but three children as well and love them like his own? I thank the Lord for Bobby Johnson, my husband.

Chapter 50

My Dad and Me

By: Charlene Hardin

My dad means so much to me. He came into my life when I was ten years old. He married my mom and became a father to my brother and sister and me.

My name is Charlene Walls Hardin. I get my name from four special men. I was born Charlene Walls. I was named Charlene after my grandfather, Charles Menke. He passed away when my mom was pregnant with me. How interesting it is to think that I have DNA and traits from him that live on in me although we never got to meet.

Walls comes from my dad, Gilford "Bud" Walls. My dad loved to research family history and our family tree. I think he would have loved the companies that test your DNA and tell you your ethnicity! The name Walls was very important to him. So, I always wanted to keep that name.

Johnson, in my name, comes from the author of this book, Bobby Johnson. He is my dad, the one that came into my life at ten years old. So, two dads meant two maiden names for me.

Lastly, Hardin. I took this name when I married the man I love five years ago, Kyle Hardin. I legally changed my name so I could have my new married name and two maiden names.

Let's start from the beginning. My dad, Bud Walls, was born in 1950 in Greer, South Carolina. He served in the Army and later served in Vietnam. After the war, he met my mom, Phyllis, and married her. I am their first child. Before I was born, my dad stopped smoking, cold turkey. Smoking was a habit he picked up in the Army. When I was born, we lived in a small mobile home. My dad worked hard building a house for us. He paid for the house as it was built so we had no mortgage. He did a lot of the manual labor himself along with help from the family and some hired help for a few things.

Some memories of my dad are such little things but they make me smile. When we would stop at the little store to get gas or pick up milk, he would tell me I could pick out one thing. I would usually pick something like a ten-cent box of lemon heads. My dad would laugh because he would have picked out a candy bar, not a tiny box of sour candy. One time my parents took me to the store and let me pick out anything I wanted. I picked out a pair of toy high heels.

I remember he liked making jokes and coming up with clever things. He told me that George Washington wasn't the first president. Of course, I believed my dad. He was right. George Washington was the first president of the United States of America, but he wasn't the first president. There were presidents before him such as presidents of other countries and presidents of clubs. My teachers at school did not agree when I told them that George Washington was not the first president!

Another memory was he would hold up both hands, and would hold up his pinky that you would call the tenth finger. He said this is number 10, right? Yes, I would say. Then he would proceed to count down on that hand 10, 9, 8,

7, and 6. This is finger 6, right, he would say of the thumb. Yes. So 6 plus the 5 fingers on the other hand makes 11. He would tell me that he had 11 fingers! And I just couldn't understand that!

He liked making people smile. One of my favorite memories is hearing my mom and dad in his office talking about going out of town to Gatlinburg that weekend. I heard them and begged them to let us go. I just loved it so much because it was spontaneous!

My dad was a preacher at Barton Memorial Pentecostal Holiness Church. I remember him working on sermons. Although I don't remember hearing those sermons, I do remember seeing a sticky note on the wall above the steps you go down to leave the house. It had Matthew 6:34 written on it, *"Therefore do not worry about tomorrow, for tomorrow will worry about its own things. Sufficient for the day is its own trouble."* NKJV.

My dad got sick in 1992. We found out he had a brain tumor. In the war, he had been around Agent Orange, but we don't know if that is why he got brain cancer. As a little girl, ten years old, I began to pray for my dad. All day long, I would pray silently, under my breath. Sometimes you could hear me. It probably sounded like I was talking to myself. My dad died that year. He was 42 years old. That's the age I will be on my next birthday.

When my dad was sick in the hospital, one of the other local pastors visited him. That man later became my dad, Bobby Johnson. His wife had also passed away from cancer. She was sick for a very short time. The Lord brought us

"Daddy Bobby" and my dad that died became "Daddy Bud." Both of my dads were preachers.

Daddy Bobby would drive us to school and recite Psalm 23 and the Lord's Prayer on the way. He does that now with his granddaughter. Growing up, I would hear him praying and saying the names of our family and extended family and many other people. He would pray at home, at church, and in hotel rooms on vacation.

My dad always pushes and thinks forward. When I was 16, my parents bought me a brand-new Ford Ranger. Later when I was older, he pushed me to save for a car I really wanted. I am not a saver. My dad said if I would save $5,000 then he would contribute $5,000. He asked me so many times if I had my $5,000 saved yet. I did make sacrifices to save. When I say sacrifices, I mean little things like not going out to eat and not spending money on pricey coffee drinks, and especially clothes! If he would not have pushed me, I probably would not have been able to buy my dream car, a new Dodge Challenger. When I finally saved my part of the money, I was taking my time researching and trying to find the right car with the options I wanted at the right price. Then it hit me. I wanted to buy the car right away.

It was Christmas Eve, and I can still envision Mom and Dad and me sitting at Waffle House. I told my dad about a car I found. It was in Fort Mill, about an hour and a half away. I wanted to go right away, that day! My dad told me all of the things he had to do including going to the grocery store in preparation for our Christmas Eve meal. I asked if it was too much to go that day. He told me it was. I responded with, "Can we go anyway?"

So, we headed to the grocery store with my mom and got what we needed for dinner. Then, my dad and I headed to Fort Mill and bought the car. When the salesman was talking to me, my dad told him that we were in a hurry and we had to be home by dinner for our Christmas Eve meal. And, we were!

Another thing that most people know about my dad is he doesn't mess around! That is one of my favorite memories. Not buying the car but asking my dad if we could go and him agreeing. I loved that it was spontaneous! I knew it was too much, but I asked anyway because I knew he loved me and was excited for me, and liked to do good things for me.

My dad also pushed me to get a degree. I got my degree and worked in an architecture firm after college. I'm not sure if I would have gotten my degree without my dad pushing me.

When I was later laid off, I began working at a golf course. We lived in the neighborhood of this course. We really bonded when we started playing golf together and we have for many years. I worked there for about 15 years. I enjoyed working there. It gave me a very flexible schedule. My dad and I got to play a lot of golf. When I would think about getting another job, one thing I would think is that I wouldn't get to play as much golf with my dad. All those years I worked at the golf course, I was glad I had my degree because it was an accomplishment and hard work. But, I wasn't really using my degree.

Later, a great opportunity for a job came up. The job was not in my field but you had to have a degree to be eligible for the job. Without it, I would not have gotten the job. I am so thankful for my dad pushing me to get that degree. It seems like the Lord just worked it out for me. I got the job, and it has a very good schedule. It also more than doubled my salary. Of course, I wasn't working at the golf course to make a lot of money!

My dad is giving to people. When he was Chairman of the South Carolina World Missions Board, I traveled around with him all over the state on weekends. He was supposed to raise money for missions. Instead of asking for money at these churches, he would do something interesting. He would go, preach a message, and take up an offering for the Pastor's wife. Then after service, we would host a meal for everyone. My dad called it a sandwich extravaganza! We made lots of sandwiches including homemade pimento cheese. How generous. Even though my dad didn't receive an offering to go to missions, somehow he would end up raising so much for missions. In this position, my dad worked so hard and raised $90,000 at Campmeeting that year.

This is how it has been over the years. My dad gives money away. Then, he will get a call from someone saying they have some money to give him or they will ask if he can use any money. This is an important lesson. God appreciates giving.

By the way, while Daddy Bobby was serving as the state's World Missions Representative, the state's annual giving increased from $1.5 million to $3 million. When Dad and I did mission services across the state, I would drive for him (a big 1500 Dodge Ram truck).

My dads both served in the church, and I do, too. I work in the Mauldin Church of God, running the soundboard and cleaning the church. My husband does the words on the screen and the camera. When my family and I first went to Mauldin, my brother and sister and I would go clean the church on the weekends. We each had our part. As pastor's children, we all served in the church over the years.

My brother, Jesse, cleaned the church for years until after school when he began working full-time. My sister-in-law, Tori, sings in the church. My sister and brother-in-law, Chandra and Nick, taught a Sunday School class for years, every Sunday except maybe one Sunday a month. That is a lot of work. My siblings and I along with my mom served in many different ways over the years including putting up Christmas decorations, cleaning up after numerous meals, delivering meals and items to widows and people who had a death in the family, painting walls, renovating one of those parsonages on the Mauldin Church of God campground, renovated the house behind our church, going to Sam's for supplies, cooking, and probably other things I have forgotten. I didn't really think a lot about these various jobs. We just did them!

My dad never seems to get old. I think because he is so active and keeps working. He wrote two books after he retired and he is working on another one. My dad still teaches me that you have to work. You can't just sit around. He goes to his office to work. He thinks of others and does for others constantly. Of course, it is easy to sit on the sofa and watch TV all the time, but rest is more enjoyable when you have worked hard. Sometimes you have to push yourself.

It takes effort to read the Bible, to pray, to give, and to do for others. Sometimes you even have to push yourself to do fun things. You have to work for things in life like learning and saving. My dad teaches me you have to work hard – to serve, to give, to plan, to pray, and to hope.

Thank you, Dad, for all you have taught me and done for me. I love you.

Chapter 50 - Devotion

Trusting in Our Heavenly Father

(A Devotion from Charlene Johnson Walls Hardin)

1 Thessalonians 5:16-18, *"Rejoice evermore. Pray without ceasing. In every thing give thanks: for this is the will of God in Christ Jesus concerning you."*

As I talked about in the previous chapter, when I was a girl, ten years old, my dad was sick. He had brain cancer. I prayed for my dad not to die. I knew prayer was important at a young age. I must have heard the Scripture about praying without ceasing. I got in the habit of saying prayers under my breath all day long. I knew I couldn't just pray for him not to die because everyone eventually dies. So, I prayed a specific prayer that my dad would not die soon.

God did not answer my prayer. I have been so hurt and confused by this over the years, but it doesn't make me angry. God is beyond our comprehension. God is in the present and the future. I hate that my dad died and it is awful, but I wouldn't change how things worked out. God gave me another father and we had so many good times together.

Philippians 4:6-7, *"Be anxious for nothing, but in everything by prayer and supplication, with thanksgiving, let your requests be made known to God; and the peace of God, which surpasses all understanding, will guard your hearts and minds through Christ Jesus."* NKJV.

Of course, if someone we love is sick, we pray for them to get better but even in this, we don't need to worry. If we aren't careful, worry can become part of our life. We should pray instead of worry, not pray in our worry. Sometimes the things that we pray for presently are not the same things we would pray for in the future. God sees all this. God tells us not to worry. We know this, but it is hard to do. We don't like to worry because it is unpleasant. It doesn't feel good.

This isn't the only reason we shouldn't worry. Worry is fear. Fear can paralyze us. When we are paralyzed, we can miss opportunities. Worry can exhaust us. When we are exhausted, we don't have the energy to do other things that we need or want to do. So worry isn't just unpleasant, it can majorly affect our lives in a negative way.

Trust God and think about things you are grateful for instead of your problems. Instead of worrying, we can be energized. Take those opportunities for life and relationships. When we are worried about our problems, we are thinking of ourselves. We need to take time to pray for others and do for others.

1 Chronicles 16:34, *"Give thanks unto the Lord; for he is good; for his mercy* (love) *endureth for ever."*

You hear about self-care a lot. There are so many articles about self-care and things to do to make your life better. I've read so many times to be grateful. These aren't Christian articles, just people trying to be happier. How much more grateful should we be if we are Christians with a loving heavenly Father.? We can easily focus on all the negatives and forget about all the positive things. We have to be intentional about seeing the positive things and thanking people, and most of all, thanking God.

Chapter 51

Praise Cathedral

By: Tommy Harvey

On Sunday morning, October 2, 2022, I had the opportunity to share my perspective of the history of Praise Cathedral at the 40th Anniversary Celebration because I was there forty years ago when the church started. Although I was there when the church began, it doesn't mean that I have the definitive perspective on the church's history; nor does it mean that I have the final perspective or the all-encompassing perspective on the church's history. It simply means that my perspective is *my* perspective, and my perspective has changed as the years have gone by.

In late spring of 1982, a church business meeting was conducted on a Sunday afternoon at the Greer Church of God. The meeting was in response to a petition that had been circulating among church members regarding a new mission in the Greer area. During the meeting, the State Overseer asked, "How many people here want to start another church?" He gave no details concerning the church – no mention of a pastor, a location, or a date. He just asked a simple question.

Among those gathered, twenty-three people raised their hands. The Overseer responded, "So it's not the main body; it's just the *fringe*." As history would have it, the "fringe" met in July 1982 with eighty-five people in a rented storefront at the Country Plaza across from Tab's Flea Market in Greer and eventually organized as an official church in October of that same year.

Forty years later, the "fringe" has grown to 3066 members; encompasses 53.5 acres of land; has more than 200,000 ft^2 of buildings; is appraised at more than $30 million dollars; and has given nearly $13 million dollars to missions in its 40-year history. Today, it is officially known as Praise Cathedral Church of God. "Not bad for the 'fringe'."

When the church began, I was a junior in high school. I really didn't have much of a perspective. I was more interested in girls, and cars, and having enough money in my pocket to enjoy both than I was in what was happening with this new church mission. But over the years, a more mature perspective has emerged due to time, understanding, contemplation, and being willing to ask questions and listen. My perspective of Praise Cathedral, from its beginnings to the present date, is simply this: Praise Cathedral is a church that welcomes and embraces those who have squandered their lives on prodigal living and found themselves in the pig pen of life; having come to their senses, they return to the Father's house and are met by a family who celebrates their return. Let me explain what I mean by that statement.

"Then all the tax collectors and the sinners drew near to Him to hear Him. And the Pharisees and scribes complained, saying, "This Man receives sinners and eats with them."

So He spoke this parable to them, saying: "What man of you, having a hundred sheep, if he loses one of them, does not leave the ninety-nine in the wilderness, and go after the one which is lost until he finds it? And when he has found it, he lays it on his shoulders, rejoicing. And when he comes home, he calls together his friends and neighbors, saying to them, 'Rejoice with me, for I have found my sheep which was lost!' "I say to you that likewise there will be more joy in heaven over one sinner who repents than over ninety-nine just persons who need no repentance."

Or what woman, having ten silver coins, if she loses one coin, does not light a lamp, sweep the house, and search carefully until she finds it? "And when she has found it, she calls her friends and neighbors together, saying, 'Rejoice with me, for I have found the piece which I lost!' "Likewise, I say to you, there is joy in the presence of the angels of God over one sinner who repents."

Then He said: "A certain man had two sons. "And the younger of them said to his father, 'Father, give me the portion of goods that falls to me.' So he divided to them his livelihood. And not many days after, the younger son gathered all together, journeyed to a far country, and there wasted his possessions with prodigal living. But when he had spent all, there arose a severe famine in that land, and he began to be in want. Then he went and joined himself to a citizen of that country, and he sent him into his fields to feed swine. And he would gladly have filled his stomach with the pods that the swine ate, and no one gave him anything. But when he came to himself, he said, 'How many of my father's hired servants have bread enough and to spare, and I perish with hunger! I will arise and go to my father, and will say to him, "Father, I have sinned against heaven and before you, and I am no longer worthy to be called your son. Make me like one of your hired servants."' And he arose and came to his father. But when he was still a great way off, his father saw him and had compassion, and ran and fell on his neck and kissed him."

"And the son said to him, 'Father, I have sinned against heaven and in your sight, and am no longer worthy to be called your son.' "But the father said to his servants, 'Bring out the best robe and put it on him, and put a ring on his hand and sandals on his feet. And bring the fatted calf here and kill it, and let us eat and be merry; for this my son was dead and is alive again; he was lost and is found.' And they began to be merry."

"Now his older son was in the field. And as he came and drew near to the house, he heard music and dancing. So he called one of the servants and asked what these things meant.

"And he said to him, 'Your brother has come, and because he has received him safe and sound, your father has killed the

159

fatted calf.' *"But he was angry and would not go in. Therefore his father came out and pleaded with him.*

"So he answered and said to his father, 'Lo, these many years I have been serving you; I never transgressed your commandment at any time; and yet you never gave me a young goat, that I might make merry with my friends. But as soon as this son of yours came, who has devoured your livelihood with harlots, you killed the fatted calf for him.' "

"And he said to him, 'Son, you are always with me, and all that I have is yours. It was right that we should make merry and be glad, for your brother was dead and is alive again, and was lost and is found.' " Luke 15:1 ff.

Some of the first new people to start filling the pews of this church were prodigal sons and daughters. They were people who were reaping the consequences of poor decisions in life and wanted to return to the Father's house but knew that because of their past, they were either unwelcomed at other churches or would be treated as second-class citizens in the kingdom of God.

They believed that if they didn't look just right or act just right or follow certain rules; if they had a shady past or a criminal record or had been divorced and remarried, they could sit on the pew and make financial contributions, but they would never truly be part of God's church. Praise Cathedral just did not believe that way.

The people of Praise Cathedral believed:

- *"If anyone is in Christ, he is a new creation; old things have passed away; behold all things have become new."* 2 Corinthians 5:17.
- *"God has sent forth the Spirit of His Son into your hearts, crying out, 'Abba, Father!' Therefore, you are*

no longer a slave but a son, and if a son, then an heir of God through Christ." Galatians 3:7.

Up until this part of my life, I had grown up with an understanding that being part of the Church of God meant not only being saved and believing the Bible, but also strict adherence to a long list of rules and regulations, some of which were more strict than the Bible itself. Holiness, and sometimes salvation itself, was measured by how well one kept the rules. What I learned was that you could keep the rules and have no love for God or neighbor. You could keep the rules and hate other people, lust after your neighbor, be greedy after money, or be filled with pride and arrogance. What I learned was that holiness and harshness towards people went hand in hand; holiness and haughtiness were the warp and the woof of the fabric of Christianity. This is the very issue Jesus had with the Pharisees. He said,

"These people draw near to Me with their mouth and honor Me with their lips, but their heart is far from Me." Matthew 15:8.

"You are like whitewashed tombs which indeed appear beautiful outwardly, but inside are full of dead men's bones and all uncleanness." Matthew 23:27.

"You cleanse the outside of the cup and dish, but inside they are full of extortion and self-indulgence." Matthew 23:25.

So, in those early days of church membership, Pastor Johnson decided to return to our roots – to the very first Church of God called Christian Union on the banks of Barney Creek near Tellico Plains, Tennessee.

On August 19, 1886, the invitation to unite with the Christian Union (later to be known as the first Church of God) was stated as follows:

"As many Christians as are here present that are desirous to be free from all man-made creeds and traditions, and are willing to take the New Testament, or Law of Christ, for your only rule of faith and practice, giving each other equal rights and privilege to read and interpret for yourselves as your conscience may dictate, and are willing to set together as the Church of God to transact business as the same, come forward."

Pastor Johnson would state, "If this was good enough for the first Church of God, it ought to be good enough for us. And here, we only have two rules: 1) love God, and 2) love people. But if you want to belong to a church that has a long list of rules for you to follow, my wife and I will take you out to eat, let you know that we love you, and help you find just such a church."

Don't think for a minute that this meant compromise. Don't even entertain the idea that standards of holiness were watered down. For the first time in my life, I heard fiery sermons on holy living from a man who had tears in his eyes. I watched a man preach against sin and admonish the lost and weep at the thought that people would plunge into hell who wouldn't repent. For the first time in my life, I learned that *holiness and love* go hand in hand and that prodigal sons and daughters who needed love and acceptance also needed older brothers and sisters to show them how to be faithful, dedicated, and obedient.

Do you know what happened? God got a hold of my heart. You see, I had been a prodigal. I had not yet made it to the pig pen, but I was on my way there. And instead of God saying to me, "Boy, you made your bed, now you're going to have to lay in it," He said, "Give Me your life and repent of your sins. Trust Me with your future, and I'll direct your path." As Paul said in Romans 2:4, *"The goodness of God [led me] to repentance."*

But God not only got a hold of my heart, He got a hold of many of people's hearts in the greater Greer area. I don't know everyone's story, but I know enough. I know that some of the people who make up the membership of Praise Cathedral came to God when they were either on their way or already in the pig pen of life. I know others who criticized the work that God was doing in those early days and said they would never come to Praise Cathedral. Some of those same people also make up the membership of Praise Cathedral – even serve on staff - All worshipping together, prodigals and elder brothers because the Father had called us all inside the house to celebrate when that which was lost is found.

Reflecting on 40 years of history at Praise Cathedral, one of our more recent members shares her testimony of what this church means to her:

"Our family has been attending Praise Cathedral for almost 8 years, and I honestly don't know where we would be right now if we had never come to this church.

Shortly after we started attending, my world was turned upside down, and I found myself as a single mom trying to raise three sons pretty much on my own. I had no job, no money, and my sons and I had no stable place to live. Through church members, I was able to find and start a job in a local grocery store, but I was only making eight dollars an hour. I had borrowed money from family members to buy a very small mobile home, but it was in very poor condition... the roof leaked, there were huge rotten holes in the floor, no appliances, no heat or ac, and our only source of water was a garden hose that we had run from the outside through the bathroom window. We lived like that for four months. When the church found out, they helped us in ways that I never would have imagined possible, and provided a safe home for us that we enjoyed living in for several years.

We weren't just helped materially by Praise Cathedral, but our lives were also transformed spiritually through the amazing sermons, Bible studies, and other programs that we got involved in. There were so many Sunday morning sermons that felt like God was speaking directly to me. I had grown up in a very strict religious school and church and had never really learned of God's love. Even though I had been in church my whole life, I felt like I was developing a real relationship with God for the first time in my life.

This church has done so much for us personally and for so many other people, locally and worldwide, and it has been amazing to watch how God has in return blessed this church. We have watched the congregation continue to grow, we have seen God's amazing financial blessings on this church, we have seen the Family Life Center be built and open, we have seen and heard of the expansion of various programs here and overseas, we have seen so many special guests come to the church (including getting to meet two of my personal heroes, Dr. James and Shirley Dobson), and we have had the pleasure of watching so many others be able to grow in Christ.

I will never forget a few years ago when I was in physical therapy, recovering from my back surgery, and I struck up a conversation with another woman there who was also recovering from surgery. I told her where I went to church, and she responded, "Praise Cathedral? That church holds a special place in my heart. Those people are the real deal." She told me about how her children's father was in prison, and one Christmas she didn't have any money for presents, and Praise Cathedral stepped in and gave their family not just presents, but a Christmas meal and groceries. That is a reputation that not too many churches these days can have. I am so grateful to be able to be a part of this church. Thank you, Praise Cathedral for showing the world the love of God. Happy 40th anniversary! I can't wait to see what the next 40 will bring."

The mission statement of Praise Cathedral sums up its history and hopefully directs its future. Praise Cathedral is a family that expresses to prodigals and elder brothers a *Passion for God, Compassion for People*.

Chapter 52

I Can See Clearly Now

Principles from the Life of Joseph
Sermon Outline
Gerald Funderburk

Text: Genesis 50:18-20, *"And his brethren also went and fell down before his face; and they said, Behold, we be thy servants.*

And Joseph said unto them, Fear not: for am I in the place of God? But as for you, ye thought evil against me; but God meant it unto good, to bring to pass, as it is this day, to save much people alive."

Introduction
- o Elijah and Elisha have long been a favorite to preach about
- o David is an intriguing personality, after God's heart
- o None is more moving and Christ-like than Joseph

I.   Nothing in his family life predicted his rise to greatness

    A. Raised in a life of **NEGATIVES**
       1. Jacob: a father that was a polygamist, with 4 wives
       2. 10 stepbrothers, born of 3 competitive mothers
       3. Grandfather Laban and Dad Jacob were schemers
       4. Ruben committed incest with one of his dad's wives
       5. He was a "Daddy's Boy" bringing bitterness

6. Simeon and Levi brutally slaughtered the men of Shechem
7. Judah had a child with his daughter-in-law

*** **IT WAS THE 'DAYS OF JOSEPH'S LIFE'** ***

B. Today he would be a prime candidate for alcohol, divorce, drugs, or even a presidential candidate.

*** **HOW DID HE MAKE IT** ***
The grace of God for God was with him.

II. Joseph made the **Right Choices**

A. Country singer, George Jones, almost died in a 1999 car crash.
B. But for the Grace of God and prayers of Vestal Goodman.
C. His next album was titled "Choices"
D. Lyrics: "I'm living and dying with the choices I've made."

*** **ALL OF LIFE IS MADE UP OF CHOICES** ***

III. Joseph had **Principles**

Genesis 37:5 *"And Joseph dreamed a dream, and he told it his brethren: and they hated him yet the more."*
  o Teenage excitement – lack of judgment and wisdom
  o Matthew 7:6 *"Neither cast ye your pearls before swine"*
  o This was some 20 years before the famine
  o God was setting in motion a plan through his dream

IV. Joseph had **Dream Killers**

    A. Family, friends, misunderstandings, rejection, mockery, criticism

    B. David's brothers thought the giant was too big; David thought "He's so big I can't miss him."

    C. Numbers 23:19 *"God is not a man, that he should lie; neither the son of man, that he should repent: hath he said, and shall he not do it? or hath he spoken, and shall he not make it good?"*

V. Joseph chose **Endurance, Courage, and Patience**

    A. He experienced hatred, envy, slavery, false accusations, prison, ingratitude

    B. How did he survive? He didn't play the blame game or chose the victim.

       o It's as old as the Garden, Adam blamed Eve, Eve blamed the snake, and the snake didn't have a leg to stand on.

       o He didn't "let the mess around him get in him."

    Genesis 39:23 *"The Lord was with him, and that which he did, the Lord made it to prosper."*

VI. Joseph chose **Personal Purity**, over the pleasures of sin

    A. He could have assimilated into Egyptian culture

    B. Nothing kills dream, shipwreck lives, and withholds the hand of God's blessings more than lack of personal purity

    C. Genesis 39:9 *"How then can I do this great wickedness, and sin against God?"*

VII.   Joseph chose **Faithfulness** in all his responsibilities

    A. Genesis 39:22 *"The keeper of the prison committed to Joseph's hand all the prisoners that were in the prison."*

    B. Psalm 91:14 *"Because he hath set his love upon me, therefore will I deliver him: I will set him on high, because he hath known my name."*

    C. Missionary Fredrick Nolan, North Africa – Fleeing from enemies, he fell exhausted into a small cave about 6 feet deep and awaited sure death. He watched as a spider began to weave a web over the entrance. The enemy came, saw the web, then moved on by knowing he could not have been in the cave. Nolan later wrote:

        "Where God is as a spider's web is like a wall."

VIII.   Joseph chose a **Forging Heart**

    A. The ones that should have loved the most treated him the worse

    B. A picture of Jesus – John 1:11 *"He came unto his own and his own received him not."*

    C. 1 Peter 2:23 *"Who, when he was reviled, reviled not again."*

    D. A little girl sat at the feet of her grandmother watching her cross-stitch. She wondered why her grandmother was making such a jumbled mess of threads. Then, grandmother turned it over and she saw the finish of all her labors.

Genesis 45:1-5 **"I Can See Clearly Now"**

IX. Joseph chose to **Close the books on the past**

    A. This is not easy, especially if you nurse your wounds

    B. Forgiveness is not "Divine Amnesia"

    C. You must choose not to talk about it and keep it alive

    D. Being a prisoner of Pharaoh was not as bad as being a prisoner of his past, in his mind.

The Past Can Be:

- A <u>Museum</u> – you visit its hall, remember the past, and stop living today; dreams die
- A <u>Mausoleum</u> – a place of death. The past will smell up your life, dreams will die, and promises go unclaimed
- A <u>Mentor</u> – a place to learn, correct your mistakes and be blessed

X. Joseph chose to **Believe the promise till his dying day**

    Genesis 50:24-25 *Joseph said unto his brethren, I die: and God will surely visit you, and bring you out of this land unto the land which he sware to Abraham, to Isaac, and to Jacob . . . and ye shall carry up my bones from hence."*

    <u>"*I may not see it, but I will die with the promise in my heart.*</u>"

Song: Bye and Bye, when the morning comes.
        When all the saints of God are gathered home.
        We shall tell the story of how we overcome.
        We will understand it better bye and bye.

Chapter 53

My Dad and Me

By: Bobby Johnson

My dad was born June 12, 1914, in lower Florence County near the township of Lake City, South Carolina. He was the son of Simion B. Johnson and Viola Barfield Johnson.

He was raised on a farm with four brothers and six sisters. His mother was a Godly woman from her youth. His dad was a kind man but loved his booze.

As a young man, he felt that there was more in life than a tobacco and cotton farm. So, he and several of his brothers and cousins decided to find another way of life. They had heard about a little town called Fort Mill, South Carolina, where some cotton (textile) mills were in operation. The little town was 120 miles from Lake City.

Upon hearing about Springs Cotton Mills in Fort Mill, they began to talk among themselves. After a few months passed, several of them decided to make a venture. They walked from Lake City to Fort Mill, 120 miles. Upon their arrival at Fort Mill, they found meager lodging, very meager; they applied for jobs in the cotton mill; they were hired. So, they went from the cotton farm to the cotton mill. The young men were hard workers and soon made advancement in the mill working their way up the ladder.

The highlight of their lives was the finding of the Fort Mill Church of God. The young crowd could be rowdy sometimes, but their mother made sure that they knew something about church. They grew up attending the Camp Branch Free Will Baptist Church and later The Camp Branch Pentecostal Holiness Church of Lake City. The two churches were located across the road from each other.

The Fort Mill Church of God, located across the railroad tracks behind Culps Ice House, was organized on September 27, 1931, with nineteen members. The young group of men found that little church and joined the congregation.

The next thing on their agenda was finding young women. Each of them found a young woman and married her. All of them were Fort Mill girls. My dad married Lillie Mae Patterson who also worked in the mill and resided on Doby Bridge Road about eight miles south of Fort Mill. His wife became my mother.

My dad and mother were not strong Christians in their young days, so they drifted from the Lord and church, but after a brief time in sin, they realized their need for the Lord and the church. They became grounded in the Lord and established in the church for the rest of their lives. They birthed and raised five children. Every one of the children became church children and members of the Fort Mill Church of God.

My dad knew about "holiness", as it was called from Lake City life. Not only was his mother a Godly woman, but his granddad, Aft Barfield, was an ole-timey Godly man. His granddad would walk the dusty roads of Lake City praying for sick people and their ailing animals. He was also influenced by his Uncle Harvey and Uncle Fred Barfield in the "Way of Holiness".

My mother did not know anything about the "Holiness Way" when she married my dad, and she had a little difficulty getting adjusted to such. She was disfellowshipped from the church two times for cutting her hair. In fact, in those days, almost everything was wrong. Each time, she rejoined the church. Now it seems that a person can do almost anything and be a leader in the church. Well, that is enough of that foolishness! We survived!

My dad and mother birthed and raised four girls – Betty Ray, Patricia Ann, Sara Lee, and Joyce Marie – and one boy. They named me Bobby. Although I spent much of my growing-up days on Pawpaw's farm located on Doby Bridge Road, I was never far from the influence of loving parents and the "Holiness Way" of life.

Daddy became an outstanding leader in the Fort Mill Church of God during his lifetime. He served on almost every church committee and board and was the Sunday School Superintendent for many years. My dad was not highly educated but could converse with physicians, attorneys, and businessmen without reluctance. As a master mechanic, he could fix or repair anything. One time he joined two trucks together and made one truck. People could not believe it!

My dad was also a builder. He resided in mill village houses in Fort Mill for about 18 years after arriving there. Then he purchased some acreage on Hensley Road, about three miles south of Fort Mill, just off Doby Bridge Road. He then built his own house and resided there for more than fifty years. He also built a house for his parents on his property.

Other buildings he built included a service station and store for his son-in-law, Elmer Totherow, a country store for my granddad on Doby Bridge Road, a country store for me on Hensley Road, and participated with other church members to build their church building on Academy Street in Fort Mill, South Carolina. He witnessed more than seventy-five relatives join the Fort Mill Church of God, the second largest Church of God in South Carolina, and one of the strongest in the denomination. So, he was a spiritual builder also.

Above all that, he was used mightily in church services, walking the aisles, shedding tears, and praying for people. He became a Bible-reading man and a fervent seeker of the Lord. He loved his church, supported his Pastor without any reservation, enjoyed camp meetings, and was delighted to be in church services with me, his boy preacher. He was also honored to serve on the church's State Layman's Board for six years.

My dad was a very tender-hearted man; a man of tears, but steadfast and unmovable in the faith of our Lord Jesus Christ. He was much like Caleb of old.

Like Caleb, he could 'still' the church folk. Caleb was one of the twelve men who was sent by Moses to check out the land that the Lord had promised to give his children, the children of Israel. Ten men returned with a fearful report that dismayed and disturbed the people, the congregation of Israel. They lifted their voices; they cried out; they wept all night; and, they murmured exceedingly. In the Book of Numbers, Chapter 13, Verse 30, the Bible says, *"And Caleb stilled (quietened) the people before Moses."*

My dad was a church peacemaker, he had the God-given ability to still the people.

On one occasion, his pastor got into financial trouble. His financial difficulty could have destroyed him, and his ministry, and caused harm to the church. But my dad stood in the gap and used his influence to save the pastor. That pastor rebounded and is now a leader in the general church. Time and time again my dad, as a peacemaker, helped to keep harm from the Fort Mill Church of God.

Like Caleb, he was devout, earnest, and sincere.
Like Caleb, he was dedicated and concerned.
Like Caleb, he was diligent, persevering, and continuing.

My dad understood that there was no reward without labor; that there was no rest without a journey; that there was no victory without warfare.

He ran until he reached his goal; he fought until his crown was won; he persevered until his possession was obtained.

Believing these things about my dad encourages me, inspires me, and motivates me to continue until I hear the words that he has already heard, "Well done, my child – welcome home – a crown you have won."

This poem fits my dad:

Live the Christian life
Men will admire you
Women will respect you
Little children will love you
And God will crown your life with success.
When the twilight of your life
Mingles with the dawn of eternity,
Men will speak your name

With honor and baptize your Grave with tears
As God attunes for you the evening chimes.

My dad, above all things, was a Christian:
    The tenderness of his spirit
    The softness in his voice
    The meekness in his walk
    The kindness in his actions
    The love in his expressions
    Gave indisputable evidence,
    My dad lived a Christian life.

I completely surrendered my life unto the Lord at the age of 18 years. Shortly thereafter, the call to preach came into my spirit. At that time, I was working in Springs Cotton Mill and enrolled in Rock Hill Commercial College. It was my desire to become an accountant. I shared the feeling to preach with my dad, but he did not encourage me to become a minister of the Gospel. A few months expired. I left the mill and college and enrolled in Lee College, Cleveland, Tennessee.

When my dad saw my sincerity and my preparation for the ministry, he had a talk with me. He informed me that God had called him into the ministry, but that he pleaded unto the Lord to release that calling and to place it upon me, his son. My dad's education was very limited. He also had started a family, so he gave me to the lord and supported me without any hesitation. My calling has been for two – my dad and me. Read my book, "Taking A Chance With God."

At 89 years of age, my dad encouraged me to take another planned mission trip. He passed away while I was on that trip to the Dominican Republic. His encouraging words to me concerning my World Missions work – "Go, son, build a bridge." One day while on a trip I stood on that huge platform at the Suez Canal and watched the passing of a huge ship through the canal from one giant ocean to another, the words from my dad sounded again, "Go, son, build a bridge." We built bridges together.

My ministry has also been his ministry. My calling has also been his calling. My results have also been his results. My accomplishments have also been his accomplishments. My recognition has also been his recognition. My reward will also be his reward. For sixty-five years, I have carried my dad's spirit in my heart. For almost 20 years, I have carried his picture and funeral Order of Service in my Bible.

I refer again to my book, "Taking A Chance With God." The book contains my 65 years of full-time ministry which includes serving as Pastor of nine different churches, helping to start/plant more than 40 new churches, building more than 50 buildings from the ground up in the Church of God, serving as the SC State Director of Evangelism and Home Missions, being the youngest minister to ever serve on the SC Church of god State Council, building the strongest Church of God in South Carolina and one of the strongest and largest in our denomination (Praise Cathedral). While I was serving as the Chairman of the SC Church of God World Missions Board the state's world missions offering increased from 1.5 million annually to a record of 3 million. The spiritual results of hundreds being saved from their sins, sanctified, filled with the Holy Ghost, baptized in water, and added to the Church of God are also credited to him, my dad.

To God be the glory for calling my dad and me and using us together in His Kingdom work.

Chapter 54

Home and Family

By Bobby Johnson

Home – what magic power!

Home:
    The place where one lives (resides)
    The place (city, state, etc.) where one was born or reared
    The household or life around it

When we hear the word 'home' our mind usually goes back across the years, and for some of us, across hundreds of miles of intervening space to that place-that spot-that sight-that hillside-that old house which holds a dear and hallowed memory for us.

We are reminded of that place where we grew up as a boy or girl playing around the yard with other boys and girls – being called away from our neighboring chums – hearing our mom say, "It's supper time."

Oh, but it takes more than a place, more than a house, more than a seat, more than a defined spot, to make a home. It even takes more than a family to make a home.

The nearest thing to heaven on Earth is the Christian family and home where husband and wife, parents and children, live together in love and peace, devoted to God and to each other. By way of contrast, the nearest thing to hell on Earth is the ungodly home broken by sin and iniquity where parents quarrel and bicker and separate and where children are given over to the forces of wickedness to be brought up without Christian training and love.

The modern home is a house where members of a family meet each other in the halls occasionally on their way to some event or engagement – nothing more than a glorified rooming house.

The home is where the father can come at the end of a busy day and sit down at the supper table as an uncrowned king – honored, respected, and obeyed; and where the mother is loved, cherished, and revered as the uncrowned queen. I'll tell you, in such a home love reigns supreme and such a home is the nearest approach to heaven, that this Earth knows anything about.

The deepest longing any man can have is a longing for his home. The most dreadful disease a person can experience is homesickness. Go to the army camp and ask each soldier where he would like to be, and almost without exception, he will answer: home! Ask some prisoner in some jail cell the same question, and he will likely give you the same answer. Enter hospitals and ask the patients where they would like to be and with one voice they will answer: home! How often have you heard people say, "They cannot treat me any better here but it's just not like home. I want to go home."

Mid pleasures and palaces,
Though we may roam,
Be it ever so humble,
There's no place like home.

What really makes the home? The family.

The father, the man, Adam.

A writer penned these words, "Without man, the world would be a school without a pupil, a mansion without a resident, a temple without a worshipper, but can we even imagine Adam's failings when he stepped into life? He beheld the mountains in their grandeur; he beheld the plains and deserts with their charm. He beheld the fashioned birds and flowers with their color. He beheld the streams with their smoothness. He beheld the ocean with its forcefulness and white-capped waves. He beheld the sun with its brightness, the moon with its clearness, and the stars with their brilliance. He beheld the blossoming flowers after their kind, the singing birds after their kind, and the swimming fish as their kind. He beheld the jumping deer, the hopping rabbits, and the playful lions all after their kind.

What a place – the shining sun, the twinkling stars, the roaring ocean, the singing birds, the beautiful earth. What a place he beheld! But something was missing. God created man, for divine purposes, for man to worship the creator, to enjoy the creation, and to bless the created. But something was missing.

So the Lord said, "It is not good that the man should be alone." God Himself knew that something was lacking, as Adam stood in a great silence in the midst of a marvelous and beautiful creation. God knew that something was lacking and the all-knowing God knew what was lacking – Woman.

So God said, "I will make man a help-meet," a help-meet to develop his thinking, help-meet to cultivate his feelings, a help-meet to join him in the worship of God. Thus, woman is man's help-meet – to rejoice in his joy, to share in his sorrow, to minister to his comfort, and to aid his religious life and worship to make a home, to form a family. None of us can imagine <u>a home without a woman</u>.

Then God put the man to sleep, took a bone from his side, and made a woman. He brought her unto the man, *"And Adam said, This is now bone of my bones, and flesh of my flesh: she shall be called Woman, because she was taken out of Man. Therefore shall a man leave his father and his mother, and shall cleave unto his wife: and they shall be one flesh."* Genesis 2:23-24.

God did not take a bone from man's head for him to lord over woman. God did not take a bone from man's foot for man to kick a woman around. God took a bone from man's side for a woman to stand beside him. God took a bone from man's body for a woman to become one with him. God took a bone from near man's heart for a woman to be loved by him. God took a bone from under man's arm for the woman to be protected by him.

Thus was woman created for man. Hear Ephesians 5:21-23, *"Submitting yourselves one to another in the fear of God. Wives, submit yourselves unto your own husbands, as unto the Lord. For the husband is the head of the wife, even as Christ is the head of the church."*

Ephesians 5:33 *"Nevertheless let every one of you in particular so love his wife even as himself; and the wife see that she reverence her husband."*

Colossians 3:19 *"Husbands, love your wives, and be not bitter against them."*

Titus 2:4-5 *"Teach the young women to be sober, to love their husbands, to love their children, To be discreet,* chaste, keepers at home, good, obedient to their own husbands, that the word of God be not blasphemed."

1 Corinthians 7:3 *"Let the husband render unto the wife due benevolence: and likewise also the wife unto the husband."*

Obedience to 1 Corinthians 7:1-5 when proper submission to each other and proper love to each other will usually result in offspring.

Psalm 127:3 *"Children are an heritage of the Lord."*

Room must be made for <u>children</u>. Children, there are some Scriptures for you to consider also. Proverbs 1:8, *"My son, hear the instruction of thy father, and forsake not the law of thy mother."*

Colossians 3:20, *"Children, obey your parents in all things: for this is well pleasing unto the Lord."*

Deuteronomy 5:16, *"Honour thy father and thy mother, as the Lord thy God hath commanded thee; that thy days may be prolonged, and that it may go well with thee, in the land which the Lord thy God giveth thee."*

Now a Scripture of command to parents and a Scripture to be received by the children: Deuteronomy 6:6-7, *"And these words, which I command thee this day, shall be in thine heart: And thou shalt teach them diligently unto thy children, and shalt talk of them when thou sittest in thine house, and when thou walkest by the way, and when thou liest down, and when thou risest up."*

Every child needs to be taught diligently, and every child needs to receive what is taught.

The Husband's Prayer: *"My God and Father, how marvelous is thy plan for the fulfillment of personality and life. I thank Thee for the woman who has grown to love me and who has given herself to my keeping. Thank You for the love and affection You have given to each of us so that our hearts beat as one. Oh Lord, grant that I may continue to be worthy of my wife's trust, love, devotion, and surrender of her name. May I continue to be filled with the Christ-like spirit of thoughtfulness, unselfishness, self-control, dependability, and understanding that makes a happy marriage. Please forgive me of any deeds or words that have dimmed her eyes with tears of grief and may our years together continue to bring full blossom the love of our hearts, faithful service to Thy kingdom, and the glory of Thy Holy Name."*

The Wife's Prayer: *"Dear God, my heart is still filled with rapture and gratitude for this man who was worthy of my deepest commitment and companionship. I hope that I have proven to be a loving sweetheart; faithful helpmate, and congenial companion. I hope that my voice has not lost the tender tone that it was in courtship's smiling days. Thank You, Lord, for the wisdom that You have given to me to make home the best-loved of all places, the health to fulfill my duties cheerfully, and the grace to meet problems along the way. And dear God, when all my youthful charms have vanished, and the lines of care and age have diminished my physical attractions, may he and I be found walking hand in hand by the bond of Thy eternal love through Jesus Christ. Amen."*

I charge both husband and wife, by God's grace, ever to be true to the words of one who said:

How do I love thee?
Let me count the ways.
I love thee to the depth and breadth and
    height my soul can reach.
I love thee to the level of every day's most quiet need
    by sun and candlelight.
I love thee freely as men strive for right.
I love thee purely as they turn from praise.
I love thee with the breath, smiles, and tears of all my life,
And if God chooses,
I shall but love thee better after death.

May your home be a habitation of love and peace
forevermore.

Home, as a place,
Home, the place to be when the lightning is flashing,
Home, the place to be when the thunder is cracking,
Home, the place to be when the earth is shaking,
Home, the place to be when the hurricane is tearing,
Home, the place to be when this old world is falling apart.

Part IX

Midnight Closing

Midnight Closing

From the Ole Bishop

I woke up this morning with thoughts of closing my writings for this book. Many, many people have come to my mind today. There is no way to write about all of them. Hundreds upon hundreds have blessed me; and my ministry has reached hundreds upon hundreds, even thousands.

One of the first men that came to my mind today was Gurley Howard of Greer, South Carolina. Gurley became ill during my semi-retirement days; therefore, I was able to spend time with him during his final days. One day as I sat by his bedside, I was overcome with tears of thanksgiving and emotion as I thought: This man has supported me for years. The commodious house that I own, the beautiful vehicle that I drive, the nice clothes that I wear, and the delicious food that I eat have been made possible by this man, Gurley Howard, and many like him.

I sense an overwhelming emotion as I write about him and many others tonight. The Scripture comes to mind, Hebrews 12:1, *"Wherefore seeing we also are compassed about with so great a cloud of witnesses."*

The team that I enjoyed in the SC Church of God State Office: Dickie Davis, Dot Pyeatt, A.A. Padgett, and P.H. McCarn – all have gone to be with the Lord.

My preaching friends such as Jesse Wiggins, Orville Hagan, and P.H. McSwain —are now a part of that great cloud of witnesses.

I have seen many today in my mind who helped to compose that great cloud of witnesses: the Emanuels and others from the Latta Church of God; the Coopers, Campbells, Johnsons, and Causeys from the Mullins Church; the Bradberrys and others from the New Ellenton Church; the Clardys, McKees, Holidays, and Smiths from the Liberty Church; the Barrentines, Jones, Cooks, Sawyers, and Lynette Tanner whose conversion blessed many; Ronnie Starling whose young life was a bright light; the faithful Frierson family; and many others like the Jacobs, the Bennetts, and Mildred Rogers from the Florence Church; and, the Killmans, Davis', and Duncans from the Columbia Church.

The tall men of my ministry — Alton Howard, David Lundstrum, and Larry Harvey. All stood tall as family men and church men, and all stand tall in my mind today.

What a "Cloud of Witnesses"! Prayer warriors like Miles Mauldin, Roy Maxwell, and Haston Derrick whose prayers moved Praise Cathedral forward.

Widows such as Minnie Lane, Chris Boivin, Esther Whitmore, Marie Howard, Nell Carrin, Bonnie Waddell, Thelma Leopard, Pauline Chapman, Marie Lyons, and Sally Greer were faithful as a clock and so kind to me.

The first three of Praise Cathedral — John Story, Susan Barton, and Ronnie Howard —departed this life in the infancy of Praise Cathedral.

Ministry couples, such as Clyde and Helen Ogle, John and Mildred Weston, Ernest and Pearl Taylor, G.C. and Kathryn Spencer, who stepped out with the new church at Greer (Praise Cathedral).

The Caleb-spirited men such as J.B. Leverette, Jack Bentley, Frank Hawkins, Robert Davis, and Robert Gaines, whose influence helped to smooth matters in the church.

My golfing friends, Bill Moore, Jack McClure, Larry Sluder, A.C. Dempsey, and others brought excitement to my life.

Comrades in the faith such as David Sustar (Chris' Dad) and Thomas Madden (Jerry's Dad), and Charles Smith (John Smith's Dad) who all recently joined that great cloud of witnesses came to my mind, along with Wilton Scruggs, whose family attends the Mauldin Church of God.

Many, many retired ministers, who made that one more step are waiting on the cloud for the rest of us. Let me name a few: Leroy Baldwin, John Brooks, Roger Byrd, Joe Hood, Olin Martin, Stan McCarson, James Owens, Hubert Orvin, Newby Thompson, T. T. Madden, E. B. Ford, Coyt Kissiah, Bill McKee, Lee Black, Carl Breazeale, Sergio Burgos, and Leamon Cagle, one of our former Mauldin Church of God pastors who was pleasant to have around, along with Carroll Ellison, an award-winning musician and percussionist.

Senior Ministers such as Walter Pettit, Max Atkins, C.B. Camp, and C.E. Landreth who showed me much kindness are waiting for many of the younger crowd to join that great cloud of witnesses.

Lastly, it was my privilege to conduct the funeral services of my dad and mother, Simon B. and Lillie Mae Johnson, and Phyllis' mother, Irene Menke, who are anticipating our arrival to join the "Great Cloud of Witnesses".

Now, may the Midnight Writings of the Ole Bishop be closed with Hebrews 12:1-3,

"Wherefore seeing we also are compassed about with so great a cloud of witnesses, let us lay aside every weight, and the sin which doth so easily beset us, and let us run with patience the race that is set before us,
Looking unto Jesus the author and finisher of our faith; who for the joy that was set before him endured the cross, despising the shame, and is set down at the right hand of the throne of God.
For consider him that endured such contradiction of sinners against himself, lest ye be wearied and faint in your minds."

I had a good conversation with some dear friends, J.T. and Barbara Wallace, Florence Church folk, today. I encouraged Barbara to write a book about her family (My Family and Me). It would be very interesting.

Why don't you start some "Midnight Writings"? Someone like me will read them.

Good Night!
The Ole Bishop

Made in the USA
Middletown, DE
08 June 2023

31899631R00108